GEOGRAPHY
Province to Province

By Donna Ward
Illustrated by Marj Cassidy

DONNA WARD
NORTHWOODS PRESS

Special thanks to:
Marj Cassidy. Your sacrifice and time invested is so appreciated.
Special thanks to my family: Doug, Natalie, Jeremy, Stephanie, and Darcy
for trooping around the east coast with me,
and supporting all my hours at the library.

Other Publications by Donna Ward:
Canada, My Country (Social Studies for Early Grades)
Canada's Natives Long Ago (Native studies for Elementary Grades)
Courage and Conquest, Discovering Canadian History (Pre-Confederation history for Elementary Grades)
Africa, A Land of Hope (Social Studies for Elementary Grades)

Cover Design:	Adam Duguay, Images
Photograpy Credits:	p.8 - ClickArt 65,000, Broderbund Software, Inc.: p. 10 - ClickArt 65,000: p. 17 - ClickArt 65,000: p. 18 - ClickArt 65,000: p. 21 - ClickArt 65,000: p. 22 - ClickArt 65,000, p. 24- Marj Cassidy: p. 56 - ClickArt 65,000: p. 68 - Marj Cassidy: p. 76 - Marj Cassidy: p. 79 - Donna Ward: p. 90 - Donna Ward: p. 93 - Donna Ward: p. 96 - Donna Ward: p. 101 - ClickArt 65,000: p. 104 - Heather Shea: p. 109 - Marj Cassidy
Illustrations:	All provincial flowers, birds, shields by Marj Cassidy Illustrations by Marj Cassidy: p. 32, 41, 59, 67, 75, 83, 108, Historical boxes Other: author's adaptions from ClickArt 65,000
Acknowledgements:	Kind permission to use provincial/territorial shields granted by each provincial/territorial government respectively.

Printed and Bound in Canada
Copyright © 1999, 2007 by Donna Ward.
Revised Editions: 2000, 2007
Published by:Donna Ward/Northwoods Press
         www.donnaward.net

Canadian Cataloguing in Publication Data

Ward, Donna, 1958-
   Geography: province to province

Rev. ed.
ISBN 0-9686788-3-1

1. Canada - Geography - Juvenile literature. I. Cassidy, Marj, 1929-. II. Title.

FC58.W364 2000   971.1   C00-930711-7
F1008.2 W28 2000

Table of Contents

Economics: The Mystery of Money 4
    Lesson 1:Goods and Services
    Lesson 2:Industry
    Lesson 3:Trade and Transportation
    Lesson 4:Canada and the World

People: The Heart of Our Country 11
    Lesson 5:Population

Geography: The Shape of the Land. 14
    Lesson 6:Political Map
    Lesson 7:Geological Regions
    Lesson 8:Natural Regions
    Lesson 9:Drainage Basins

British Columbia: The Promised Land .. 23
    Lesson 10:The Promised Land
    Lesson 11:Geography
    Lesson 12:Forestry
    Lesson 13:People and Places

Alberta: The Princess Province 32
    Lesson 14:The Princess Province
    Lesson 15:Geography
    Lesson 16:Fossil Fuels
    Lesson 17:People and Places

Saskatchewan: Canada's Bread Basket .. 41
    Lesson 18:Canada's Bread Basket
    Lesson 19:Geography
    Lesson 20:Farming
    Lesson 21:People and Places

Manitoba: The Keystone Province 50
    Lesson 22:The Keystone Province
    Lesson 23:Geography
    Lesson 24:Multiculturalism
    Lesson 25:People and Places

Ontario: Land of Sparkling Waters 59
    Lesson 26:Land of Sparkling Waters
    Lesson 27:Geography
    Lesson 28:Manufacturing
    Lesson 29:People and Places

Quebec: Place Where the River Narrows .. .67
    Lesson 30:Place Where the River Narrows
    Lesson 31:Geography
    Lesson 32:Power in the Water
    Lesson 33:People and Places

New Brunswick: The Picture Province 75
    Lesson 34:The Picture Province
    Lesson 35:Geography
    Lesson 36:Endangered Wildlife
    Lesson 37:People and Places

Nova Scotia: Canada's Ocean Playground . . .83
    Lesson 38:Ocean Playground
    Lesson 39:Geography
    Lesson 40:Fishing
    Lesson 41:People and Places

Prince Edward Island: The Island 92
    Lesson 42:The Island
    Lesson 43:Geography
    Lesson 44:Tourism
    Lesson 45:People and Places

Newfoundland and Labrador: The Rock . . . 100
    Lesson 46:The Rock
    Lesson 47:Geography
    Lesson 48:Mining
    Lesson 49:People and Places

Yukon: Land of the Midnight Sun 108
    Lesson 50:Land of the Midnight Sun
    Lesson 51:Geography
    Lesson 52:People and Places

Northwest Territories: Land of the People .. 114
    Lesson 53:Land of the People
    Lesson 54:Geography
    Lesson 55:People and Places

Nunavut: Our Land .120
    Lesson 56:Our Land
    Lesson 57:Geography
    Lesson 58:People and Places

Population Bar Graph 126
Student Work Answer Key 127

ECONOMICS THE MYSTERY OF MONEY

Do you want to be truly rich? You already are if you are happy and good. Tell those who are rich not to be proud. They should be rich in good works.

If you received some birthday money, how would you choose to spend it? Would you spend it on candy or save it for something valuable? *Economic* choices challenge each one of us. An *economist* studies how *goods and services* (the things people want to buy) are *produced* and *distributed* to the people who want them.

To economize means to make careful choices about spending.

Goods are the things we buy such as books, bicycles, and houses. *Services* refer to the work provided by people like sales clerks, auto mechanics, or the repairman who comes to fix the furnace. People usually want more than they can buy. Everyone has to make choices, including you: a gift for Mom or a new book? A family makes choices: a carpet in John's room or a ping-pong table? A country makes choices: new roads or rescue helicopters? We all have to *economize* to satisfy our most important needs and desires.

GOODS

SERVICES

Economizing with Budgeting

A budget is a plan for spending (*expenses*) the money you expect to receive (*income*). The most successful money managers are those who plan ahead.

Income: *Income* is money you earn from allowance, jobs or gifts.

Expenses: *Expenses* are what you spend your money on.

Expenses:

Charity: Just as we have been given good things, we should give to help others in need.

Savings: One should put money into *savings* for future needs, such as college education.

Needs: The things you *need* might be an item of clothing, a tool, money for phone calls, or food.

Wants: What are the things you *want*? What is the cost? What items do you want more than others (priorities)?

Lesson 1~Assignment

Using notepaper, answer this question in paragraph form. Add it to this workbook. What does it mean to *economize*? What are some bad economic choices a student might make? What are good choices students can make with their money?

Plan a budget for yourself. It can be a weekly budget, a monthly budget or a yearly budget. This depends on your income; when you receive it and how regularly you receive it.

List your expected income. You may want to brainstorm some ways to increase your income.

List your expenses including charity, savings, needs, and wants. When you list your needs and wants, list them in priority. Ask yourself: how often will I use this? Is it worth the price? Is it a tool (something useful) or a toy (just a play thing)? How long will it take you to save for it?

After you have listed these things fill in the budget chart unless your parents have another model they prefer you to use.

Total Income:	$30.00
Expenses:	
Charity	$3.00
Savings:	$18.00
Needs:	$6.00
Total	$27.00
Subtract Expenses from Income	$3.00
Wants (Do you have money left for wants?)	$3.00

Lesson 2~Assignment

Pick one of the products listed below. On a piece of lined paper write about each stage of production needed to complete the product. An example is given. When completed, include this in this your workbook.

Wooden desk   Newspaper
Clay plant pot   Loaf of bread

Example:	Cotton Drapes
Primary	• cotton is harvested
Secondary	• cotton is spun into thread and woven into cloth
	• cloth is printed with pattern
Service	• drapery store buys the cloth
	• salesman sells it to us
	• seamstress (my mother) measures the window and sews the cloth into drapes

Lesson 3~Assignment

On a lined piece of paper, make a chart with three columns. Label column one–Imports; column two–Country of Origin (where it came from); and column three–Made in Canada. Fill in the chart listing products in your home or school room. Look on the bottoms of dishes, fine china, inside books, on clothing tags, food labels, and on plastic products. Have a contest to see who can find the most countries or items.

Do you bake cookies or create craft projects? A busy, productive person is described as industrious. The root word, *industry,* means the *production* of goods and services. There are three stages of industry: *primary, secondary, and service.*

The people who work closely with nature to gather the resources of the land are involved in *primary industry.* The miner drills away at rock deep underground. Loggers trim and stack trees. The wind-burned fisherman and the sun-tanned farmer both rise early to gather the harvest. *Natural resources* such as minerals, lumber, or animals, once gathered, are called *raw material.* Canada's vast land provides a great amount of raw materials for workers in primary industries to collect.

How does that pile of rock become anything of value? In *secondary industry,* the raw materials are made into the products people want. This is the stage called *manufacturing.* In factories and mills across Canada, resources are made into these products people desire.

Firemen, store clerks, bankers and librarians also work in industry, although they do not produce goods. They provide services for others. There are more people employed in the *service industry* than those in all the other industries combined. The service industry has been divided into two groups.

1) *Tertiary industries* include the services of retail stores, medical and rescue squads, insurance companies, airlines, and repair personnel. Can you think of any other services your family would pay for?

2) The second service group, the *quaternary industries,* include all information and communication services. Medical researchers, computer technicians, and business analysts collect information in their field. Internet providers, phone and television companies provide ways to communicate the information. The quaternary industry group is the fastest growing area in the industry sector.

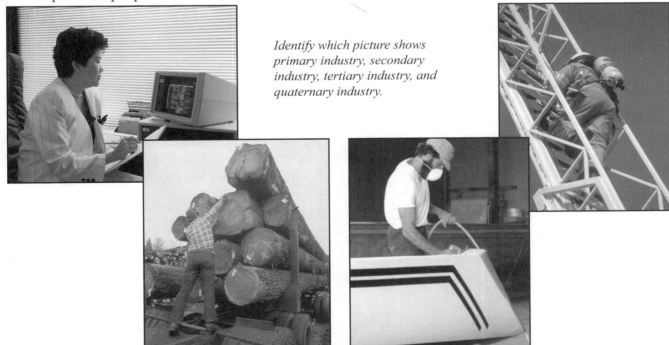

Identify which picture shows primary industry, secondary industry, tertiary industry, and quaternary industry.

Have you traded hockey cards, stickers, or stamps? Trade has been going on for thousands of years. The exchange, purchase, or sale of goods is still called *trade*. If it occurs between countries, it is called *international trade*.

One region or country may specialize in certain products because they have an advantage either in resources or knowledge. Canada has hectares of forest with trees suitable for pulp and paper. We specialize in newsprint and sell it around the world. Goods sold internationally are called *exports*. Germany has specialized in developing excellent quality toys. You may have a German-made toy in your home. Goods bought from other countries are called *imports*. International trade can provide us with both unique and less expensive goods.

Manufacturing is not distributed evenly among the provinces in Canada. Some have a wealth in one natural resource while others are rich in another. The climate, landscape and close proximity to transportation routes are factors that determine the location of manufacturers. The bulk of both primary and secondary industry, along with the population, is located along the transportation route of the Great Lakes and the St. Lawrence Seaway. This area of Ontario and Quebec is called Canada's heartland.

In a country the size of Canada, transportation is a major concern to companies distributing goods. Freight is often carried in more than one way before it reaches the market. The manufacturer looks for the least expensive transportation.

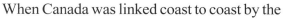

The St. Lawrence Seaway, with its access to the Great Lakes, and the seaports of our western shores, provide access for shipping. This is the least expensive but also the slowest form of moving freight.

The most commonly used carriers are trucks. Trucks are not dependent on tracks 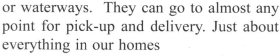 or waterways. They can go to almost any point for pick-up and delivery. Just about everything in our homes has made part of its journey to us by truck.

The quickest but most expensive method of transporting goods is by cargo airplane. Usually only small shipments are sent by air.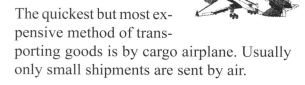

When Canada was linked coast to coast by the railway in the 19th century, transporting people and goods quickly across huge distances became a reality. The railway still moves cargo such as grain, iron-ore, and coal.

Pipelines make it possible for liquids and gases to be transported from northern drilling sites to southern markets. Building the pipeline is a costly venture, but moving liquids or gases through it is inexpensive.

Early in Canada's history, the economy depended on natural resources like furs, fish, and timber. In the 19th century, factories were built and industry became the most important job producer. Now, the highest percentage of Canadians work in service industries.

Forestry is Canada's largest industry group. Canada exports more forest products than any other country and leads the world in the production of newsprint.

Farm produce accounts for almost ten percent of Canadian exports. Wheat, the most valuable agricultural product, is followed in value by fruits and vegetables, beef, dairy products, hogs, and poultry.

Since our country is bordered by three different oceans and has many lakes, it is easy to see why our *fishing* industry is one of the largest in the world. The Atlantic fishery produces about sixty-four percent of the Canadian fishing income; the Pacific fishery about twenty-nine percent; and inland fishing the final seven percent.

Minerals, an important Canadian resource, are used in Canada and around the world. Mining companies extract nickel, zinc, copper, gold, iron ore, and many other minerals. Since the 1947 discovery of oil and natural gas in Alberta, Canada has become one of the world's major exporters of petroleum products.

Canada benefits from industry in other countries. We can import goods that we need but are not made in Canada. Some nations like Korea, Brazil, or China, pay lower wages and so produce goods at lower prices. Other countries such as Japan, Sweden, and Germany, have improved the quality of goods or developed new products through scientific research.

Canada has a strong market for her natural resources, but since the price of raw materials is dropping, critics suggest that we need to pay more attention to research and to the development of new products.

Canadians bring in only two percent of the fish caught in the oceans of the world but are the leaders in volume of fish exports. Why do you think this is? Look for the answer in Lesson 40.

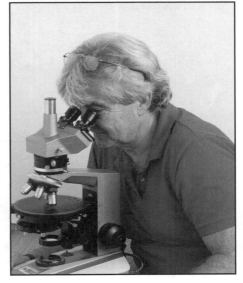

Canada needs more specialized researchers. Is this job something you might like to do?

1. Of the four questions listed, circle the one an *economist* would *not* ask.

a) How many people want to buy computers?
b) How many gold mines are there in Canada?
c) What has been the average snowfall over the last five years?
d) Were toy sales higher this year over last year?

(c is circled)

2. In the blank beside each sentence write: "P" if it describes a *primary* industry, "Sec" if it describes *secondary* industry, and "Ser" if it describes a *service* industry.

__Sec__ At the National Sea Products factory in Lunenburg, N.S., fish sticks are made, and packaged in a box with the High Liner label.

__P__ Across Canada, those in the timber trade not only harvest trees, but also finance replanting projects to provide timber for the next generation.

__Ser__ Computer software trainers help people to learn computer programs.

__P__ When oil prices went way up in the 1970s, oil producers in Alberta made a lot of money.

__Ser__ Health care workers such as doctors, nurses, and dentists, are important in every community

3. Match the definition:

Exports — to make choices about spending
Industry — goods & services exchanged between countries
Economize — products bought from other countries
Imports — the making of products
International trade — products sold to other countries

4. If a country imported more goods than it exported, would this be good for the economy? Explain your answer.

PEOPLE
THE HEART
OF OUR
COUNTRY

Prime Minister Mackenzie King, . . . made the oft repeated quip: "If some countries have too much history, we have too much geography" . . . . but here in Canada we have plenty of history. Tons. We have history to spare. It is just vastly under appreciated . . . . We have elevated real estate at the expense of history. . . . It is in the cities and towns and villages of Canada that I feel most Canadian. It is there that Canadians have shaped a culture and a way of life; in Old Quebec, in ramshackle St. John's, . . . in Victoria . . . .

Will Ferguson, *Why I Hate Canadians*
(Vancouver: Douglas & McIntyre Ltd., 1997).

Canada, the second largest country in the world, is small in population. We rank 31st after countries like China with 1.2 billion people, or India with a population of 900 million. Our 30 million hardly fills our vast land.

With an area of almost 10 million square kilometers, the *population density* in Canada is three people per square kilometre. Canadians, however, do not live spread out across the land, but clumped along our southern borders where the climate is much more hospitable than the north. Visitors to our country are amazed at the space we have, and how easy it is to reach the "land of solitude" from the populated areas.

The study of population is called *demography.* Demographers calculate:

1) *growth;* how numbers increase and decrease,

2) the *composition*; what groups of people make up a population; and

3) *patterns*; where people live and how they are distributed.

Statistics Canada, an agency of the federal government, collects and publishes facts about Canada's population. This information is useful to many groups like city planners or businesses. Information is published annually in the *Canada Year Book,* which is available in any library. How do countries calculate population? Governments conduct a *census,* or a count of the people. Taking a census of 30 million people is complicated, especially when more information is desired than just numbers. *Statistics Canada* consults with businesses and researchers to decide what questions should be included in the census. Thousands of detailed maps divide regions and cities into census tracts where questionnaires are dropped off at every household. The information received back is entered into computers, sorted, and published. In Canada, a census is taken every five years.

Population increases or decreases in two ways: through *natural change* and through *migration.* To calculate natural change, the birth rates and death rates are compared. When there are more births than deaths, there is a *natural increase* in population. Migration occurs when people move from one area to settle in another. People coming into a country are called *immigrants.* People leaving are called *emigrants.* If there are more immigrants than emigrants, does the population increase or decrease?

> **Population density is the number of people averaged over the space of an area.**

Types of Places to Live

Hamlet	5 - 800 people
Village	80-4000 people
Town	4000-20,000
Small city	20,000-100,000
Large city	100,000 - 500,000
Metropolis	500,000 - 2,500,000
Megalopolis	2,500,000 - 15,000,000

Internet Links: See the **Statistics Canada** site for a census game and outline maps including a population map, or find link directly through Easylinks at **donnaward.net**

Circle the correct answer:

1.   The population of Canada is: a. 900 million   b. 30 million.

2.   The population density in Canada is: a. 3 people per square km   b. 10 people per square km.

3.   Canada   a. is very populated   b. has a lot of space.

4.   Demography is the study of   a. statistics   b. population.

Demographers study growth, composition and patterns of population. Draw a line to match to right definition to each of these terms.

growth   what groups of people make up the population

composition   where people live and how they are distributed

patterns   how numbers increase and decrease

Down:
1. A place to live with more than 500,000 people is called...
2. A place to live with 5 - 800 people is called a ....
3. A place to live with 4000 - 20,000 people is called ...

Across:
1. People leaving the country are called...
2. People coming into the country are called.
3. The number of people in a place is called the _____ of the place.
4. A count of the people is called..

Choose from these words.
census
hamlet
emigrants
metropolis
immigrants
population
town

UNIT THREE

GEOGRAPHY
THE SHAPE OF THE LAND

The waves have a story to tell me,
As I lie on the lonely beach;
Chanting aloft in the pine-tops,
The wind has a lesson to teach;
But the stars sing an anthem of glory
I cannot put into speech.

But the stars throng out in their glory,
And they sing of the God in man;
They sing of the Mighty Master,
Of the loom his fingers span,
Where a star or a soul is a part of the whole,
And weft in the wondrous plan.

from *"The Three Voices"* by Robert Service
(first published in 1907).

Geography is exciting. If by exploring caves, studying wild animals, or discovering foreign lifestyles you learn more about the earth and the living things on the earth, you are learning geography. Geography is the study of the earth: the land, the water, and the climate. Geography is also the study of how plants, animals, and man are interconnected.

Maps produced by geographers give us many different kinds of information. A *political map* shows man-made boundaries like country borders, provinces, and cities. A *physical map* shows the earth's surface with oceans, lakes, rivers, and mountains. One kind of physical map, a *relief map*, shows the differences in the height of mountains, valleys, and plains using contour lines, colour, shading, or three dimensional dips and rises such as a globe might have. There are also road maps, weather maps, population distribution maps, and natural resources maps. If you ask a geographical question, a map may clarify the answer.

Lesson 6~Political Map

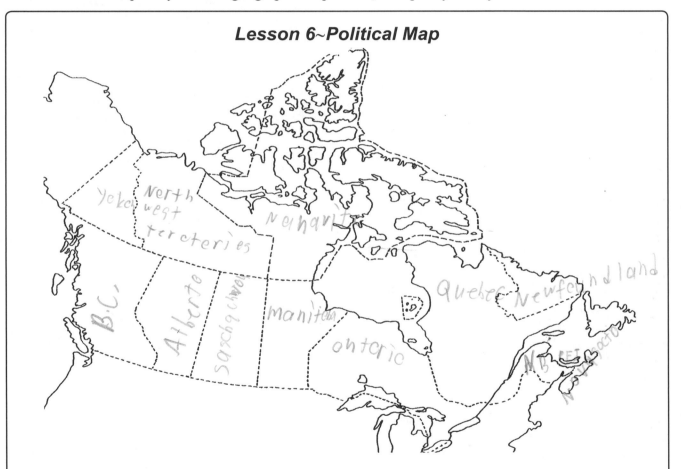

How well do you know Canada's political map? Can you name all the provinces and spell them correctly? Try identifying some lakes, rivers, and the provincial capitals. Spend the rest of this lesson reviewing and learning new facts using an atlas showing Canada's political map.

Hot Seat Game: Sit on chairs in a row facing the teacher. The teacher will call a province, and the first student who stands and gives the correct name of the corresponding provincial capital, wins a point. Turn the game around; call a provincial capital and students name the province. You can include other location names such as lakes, rivers, or major cities.

Internet Links: Visit **Sheppard Software** for fun Canada map games for all ages. Visit **Statistics Canada** for outline maps or find link directly through Easylinks at **donnaward.net**

Geology is the study of the surface of the earth especially as it relates to rocks and landforms. Geological regions are areas in which the landforms have similar characteristics. Canada is divided into eight regions: four raised regions, and four lowland areas. Canada's landscape is as varied as it is spectacular. Follow along using both the map in your workbook and a relief map found in an atlas, on a globe, or online.

Raised Regions

The western mountains, called the *Western Cordillera*, are very high, with snow-covered peaks and jagged formations. There are several mountain ranges running north and south, the most well-known being the Rocky Mountains along the BC/Alberta border. The highest mountain in Canada, Mount Logan, lies on the Yukon/Alaska border. Between the range of peaks, river valleys and plateaus there is land suitable for habitation and farming.

The *Innuitian Mountains* stretch across Canada's northern arctic islands, most notably, on Ellesmere Island. Though not as high, they look more like the Western Cordillera than any other mountainous area in Canada.

The largest region, the *Canadian Shield*, covers almost half of all the area in Canada. Rocky outcrops, spruce and pine forests, numerous lakes, rivers, and marshy bogs make up the landscape of this vast region. The cold northern climate and lack of farmland create a harsh environment unsuitable for settlement, though the southern areas of the Canadian Shield are a favourite vacation land.

To the east, the Maritime provinces and Newfoundland are part of the *Appalachian Mountains* which extend south along the east coast of North America. These rolling hills are covered in mixed forest that dazzles the eye in autumn with blazing reds and golds.

Internet Links: Photos of geological regions at **Geoscape Canada**. Geography quizzes at **Fun Trivia.** Relief maps at **Canada Info Link**. Easylink at **donnaward.net**

Unconsciously, Canadians feel that any people can live where the climate is gentle. It takes a special people to prosper where nature makes it so hard.

Robert MacNeil
Canadian born American broadcaster and writer.

I know a man whose school could never teach him patriotism, but who acquired that virtue when he felt in his bones the vastness of his land, and the greatness of those who founded it.

Pierre Eliott Trudeau
Former Prime Minister of Canada.

Lowland Regions

The *Interior Plain* includes tundra in the north, forest in the central area, and prairies in the south. Originally, the prairies were vast grasslands where buffalo herds roamed, but now fields of grain stretch to each horizon. The plains rise in three distinct levels from the lower Manitoba Plain in the east, to the highest, the Alberta Plain in the west.

South of the Innuitian Mountains, the *Arctic Lowlands* cover the rest of the northern arctic islands, and are closer to sea level than the Canadian Shield. This region is covered with ice and snow in the long winters, and with lichen in the short summers.

The *Hudson Bay Lowlands* were once part of Hudson Bay and lie flat like a lake bottom. *Muskeg,* an Algonquin term meaning 'grassy bog,' covers much of these lowlands.

The *Great Lakes and St. Lawrence Lowland* is the smallest region in Canada but the most populated. Warmer climates, level land, and fertile soil make this area valuable in fruit, vegetable, and livestock farming.

Wheat is the main grain crop of the prairies.

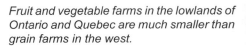

Fruit and vegetable farms in the lowlands of Ontario and Quebec are much smaller than grain farms in the west.

It is our outrageous dimensions that give shape and reason to our identity as Canadians. . . .
It takes six time zones to accommodate Canada's vast expanse, so that when it's 4:30 in the afternoon in Newfoundland, clocks are chiming high noon across the Yukon.
The land's mood, seasons and weathers are the chronometers by which we measure our lives. It is the land that anchors our sense of who we really are.

Peter C. Newman in
Canada, The Land That Shapes Us by Malek

Lesson 7~Geological Regions

Colour each geological region a different colour and put a coloured dot in the key beside the appropriate region.

Key:
- Western Cordillera
- Innuitian Mountains
- Canadian Shield
- Appalacian Mountains
- Interior Plain
- Arctic Lowland
- Hudson Bay Lowland
- Great Lakes/St. Lawrence Lowland

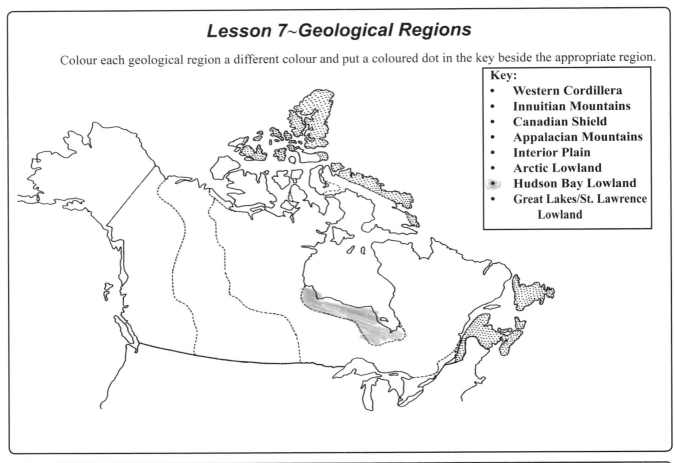

Lesson 8~Natural Regions

Colour each natural region a different colour and put a coloured dot in the key beside the appropriate region.

Key:
- Tundra
- Taiga
- Muskeg
- Boreal Forest
- Pacific Coast Rainforest
- Montaine Cordillera
- Prairie
- Aspen Parkland
- Mixed Wood Forest

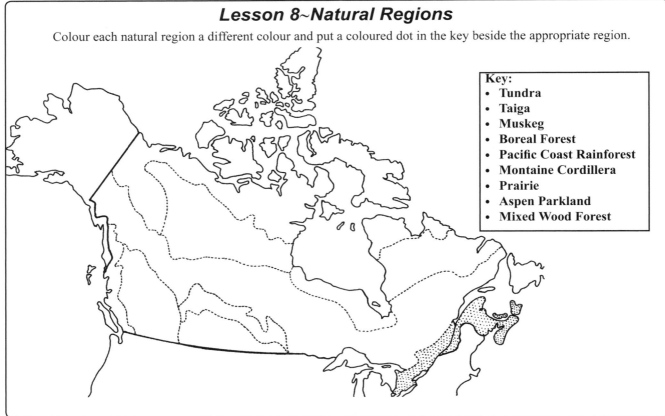

A natural region, also called a *biome* or *ecozone*, is an area where climate, vegetation, and wildlife are similar throughout the area. *Geological* regions describe the land surface such as mountains and plains, while *natural* regions define the types of trees and plants. Use the map in your notebook as you read about the natural regions.

Tundra is the harsh but beautiful land that circles the North Pole. The long, bitter winters and short, cool summers leave little time for plant growth. The ground close to the surface is permanently frozen (permafrost), hampering the development of deep roots so trees cannot survive in this climate. Shrubs, grasses, lichens, and mosses grow close to the ground. There is very little precipitation, making the Tundra like a frozen desert.

Animals that survive here, such as polar bear, muskox, caribou, arctic fox, and arctic hare grow thick coats which protect them from wind and the chill of winter. This land is often called the Barrens, or Barren Lands, because of its harshness.

South of the *Tundra* lies a transitional zone called the *Taiga*, where needleleaf trees are sparse and stunted. Below the treeline, the *Boreal Forest* stretches in a vast wilderness of spruce and pine, covering 2.5 million square kilometers. This forest provides most of our resources for pulp and paper. It supports woodland caribou, deer, black bear, lynx, coyote, bobcat, and various smaller mammals. In the mountainous area of the forest live the grizzly bear, mountain sheep and mountain goat.

The raccoon is one of Canada's most prevalent small animals, adapting well to city life.

The Red Fox gets a thicker coat in the winter time.

An abundance of rainfall and the long growing season produce lush vegetation in the *Pacific Coast Rainforest*. Cedar trees grow to enormous heights, up to 100 meters. The majority of the trees are coniferous. The ocean is home to the sea lion, seals, whales, and the sea otter. Salmon come up the coastal rivers to spawn. The bald eagle, after near extinction, is commonly seen along the coast.

The *Montaine Cordillera* is the mountainous region between the Pacific Coast Rainforest and the Prairies. The vegetation varies according to elevation. In the river valleys and plateau areas there is both fertile land and dry desert-like land that includes sagebrush and cactus. Much of the plateau is grassland. At middle elevations, the vegetation is similar to the Boreal Forest with needle-leaf trees. Below the icy mountain peaks, only lichen, moss, and shrubs survive, similar to the northern Tundra. Wildlife in the alpine areas include elk, cougar, bighorn sheep, grizzly and black bear, wolf, wolverine, and lynx.

The flat *Prairie* region originally contained grasses with long roots that could always find moisture, even in drought. Most of this early vegetation has been replaced by flat or rolling fields of grain. Before the settlers came, large herds of bison roamed the plains. These grazers are now confined to parks in the north. Today, mammals of the Prairie include deer, coyote, badger, jack rabbit, and gopher. Marshes are home to many species of waterfowl. Between the Prairies and Boreal Forest, the *Parkland* zone is a mixture of both grassy meadows and groves of trembling aspen and balsam poplar.

In the most southerly region of Canada, the *Mixed Wood Forest,* with a warm climate and plentiful rainfall, allows for more species of trees than any other zone. Deciduous trees, those which lose their leaves in winter, are predominant, producing the splendid colours so many Canadians enjoy in the fall. Prior to settlement, this area was heavily forested but less than 10% of the original forest is left because of the cities and farms that have replaced it. Fruit orchards and vegetable fields are prevalent. Few large mammals remain, but deer, raccoon, and skunk are common.

The climate of the Mixed Wood Forest is warm enough for many species of deciduous trees to grow, along with various coniferous trees. The sugar maple provides some of the brightest autumn colours.

Check your library for books about biomes:
Rebecca L. Johnson. Biomes of North America Series: *A Walk in the Boreal Forest; A Walk in the Prairie; A Walk in the Deciduous Forest; A Walk in the Tundra.* **Lerner Publications, 2001.**
Michael George, *Tundra.* **Creative Education, 1993 (wonderful photos).**

Have you ever mucked along a dirt road after a heavy rain or gotten a soaker in the ditch? A muddy road is a good picture of how rivers are formed. As little trickles join to form a main stream carrying water to the ditch, a channel is worn in the dirt. The top of a ridge is a 'watershed' and the water runs down to join in the channels and then into the larger ditch.

Rivers usually begin as small brooks high in the mountains or hills. They are joined by other streams as they tumble down, increase in size, and flow into one main river. All these *tributaries* and the river form the *river system*. The area from which waters flow toward a common destination is called a *drainage basin.*

Rivers shape the land. Turbulent waters of a cascading river can cut through rock, creating deep gorges. The fast current

All rivers flow toward the sea.

carries sand, gravel, or even heavy rock, which wears down the bed of the stream to form high banks. As a river enters land with gentler slopes, the current slows and the bed and banks are not worn down so dramatically. Without the speed, water flows around obstacles instead of through them. They collect deposits of silt until islands are formed. Very slow-moving rivers, such as prairie rivers, meander in an S-shape, depositing mud on the river bed instead of carving it out. This type of river may often flood its low banks.

The mouth of a river, where it empties into a lake or the sea, is constantly moving and changing. Some of the world's best seaports are shaped at estuaries where tides and river currents meet. Tides and waves carry away the silt deposited by the river, keeping the river mouth broad yet protected from the ocean's fury. The Gulf of St. Lawrence is a good example of a deep estuary.

When the mouth of a river is completely sheltered, sediment piles up and forms a delta. A triangular shaped island is built as silt and sand are collected and the river splits off into branches. The slower a river flows, the larger the delta will become. Canada's Mackenzie River delta is one of the largest in the world.

A fast moving tributary makes its way down to join the main channel.

Internet Links: Visit **Fun Trivia Quizzes** to test yourself on the rivers of Canada. Link directly through Easylinks at **donnaward.net**

Lesson 9~Drainage Basins

Use a blue pencil crayon to feather or outline the oceans. Then in blue, trace each major river from its source to the place where it empties into the sea. Use a red pencil crayon to outline the boundaries of each drainage basin.

1. There should be a circle around rivers that drain into the Pacific Ocean.
2. Group the rivers that drain into the Arctic Ocean.
3. The largest drainage basin includes the rivers that drain into Hudson and James Bay.
4. The final drainage basin includes the Great Lakes and rivers that drain to the St. Lawrence River and the Atlantic Ocean.

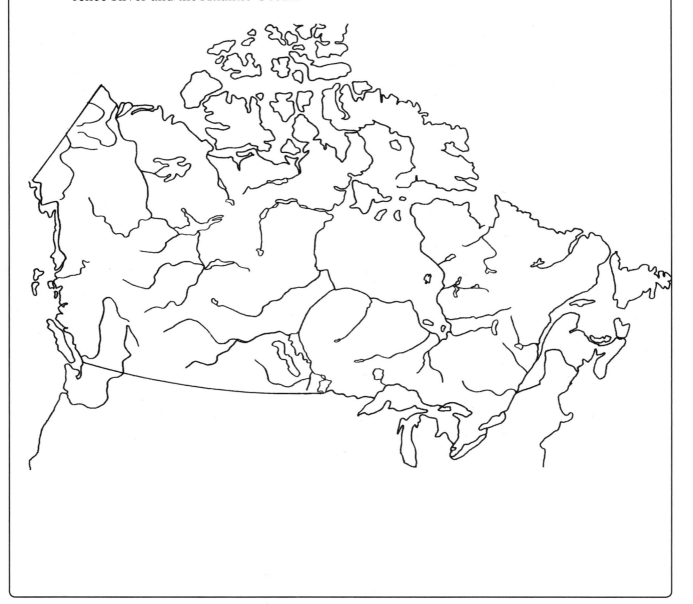

BRITISH COLUMBIA
THE PROMISED LAND

If all the world's a stage, British Columbia is one of its most dramatic sets. It is an ice-capped, forest-floored, mineral-rich, water-blessed mountain domain. It is a land of abundance, opportunity and magnificence. Untamed, restless and bold... it is a land for the young, for dreamers, doers and for those who still seek a challenging life. It is an impudent land, here cultivated, there wild, often benign, sometimes angry, always active. 'Energetic' describes it best.

Herbert L. McDonald. *British Columbia: Challenge in Abundance.*
(Canadian Confederation Centennial Committee of British Columbia, 1966).

The southern part of British Columbia was originally called Columbia, after the Columbia River. When it became a British colony in 1858, Queen Victoria named it British Columbia. On July 20, 1871, it became the sixth province to join the Dominion of Canada. Lush vegetation, a moderate climate, and incredible scenery make this a paradise for many - their Promised Land.

Steller's Jay

Screeching shatters the silence of the evergreen forest. Is the noisy Steller's Jay protecting its nest, or warning of danger? Larger than the Blue Jay, the Steller's Jay can be 30-34 centimetres long. It is the only western jay with a crest. Foraging for pine seeds and acorns in treetops, it can also rob the eggs and young of small songbirds. Its all-purpose beak can hammer, crack, probe or tear to reach its food. Steller's Jays stay year round in the coniferous forest ranging from the Pacific to the Rocky Mountains.

Pacific Dogwood

The Pacific Dogwood tree grows up to 18 meters high producing big white flowers in spring and red berries in autumn. The flower centres are yellow.

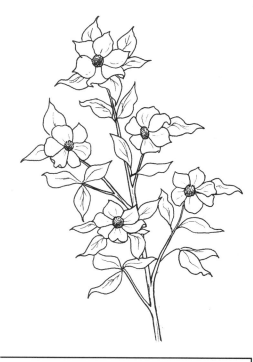

Economy

The economy of British Columbia is linked integrally to the forest industry since two-thirds of the province is forested. The generous rainfall and mild climate produce very tall, straight trees. More than 60% of Canada's lumber comes from British Columbia.

What do camels have to do with B.C.?

In 1854, camels were used to build the Cariboo Trail into the interior of B.C. Wild camels were still seen up to 1925.

Internet Links: Visit **Kids Zone** for Steller's Jay photos, information and a fun Steller's Jay Maze. Also time yourself with the Dogwood Online puzzle. Easylinks at **donnaward.net**

Research to appropriately colour each symbol.

Pacific Dogwood   **Steller's Jay**

Symbols of the Shield   **Shield**
(give the meanings of the symbols on the shield)

Union Jack: _The province's link_
whith Great Brittain

Wavy blue bars: _____

_____

Sun: _it is the most western_
province in Canada

BRITISH COLUMBIA

British Columbia has some of the most spectacular scenery and the most diverse climate of all the other provinces. The province is completely in the *Western Cordillera* region, except for a small section in the northeast corner which lies in the *Plains* region. Three groups of mountain ranges run north and south with a plateau in the centre.

The *Island Mountains* are a series of underwater peaks, some of which break the surface and form a network of islands all along the coast. Vancouver Island is the largest, and the Queen Charlotte Islands are also a large group. The islands protect the mainland from storms, creating a sheltered water passage for fishing boats.

The *Coast Mountains* extend the length of the province. They trap warm, moist air blowing in from the Pacific Ocean and keep the cold Arctic air out. These mountains keep the temperature at the coast more moderate than anywhere else in Canada: warmer in winter, and cooler in summer.

The Island and Coast Mountains together are called the *Coastal Mountains*. The natural region of this area is the *Pacific Rain Forest*. The long growing season and abundant rainfall produces lush vegetation.

Sandwiched between the coastal and interior ranges is a series of rugged, rolling hills with stretches of flat land along river valleys called the *Interior Plateau*. Fruits and vegetables are grown in the southern Okanagan Valley. North of that, grasslands provide a place for cattle to graze. Moisture, blocked by the Coast Mountains, fails to reach the plateau, so that there is far less rainfall than in the coastal areas. Some southern parts of the valleys are actually desert, with rattlesnakes, lizards and cacti.

The *Interior Mountain* region is made up of several mountain ranges. The Columbia Mountains consist of several ranges: the Cariboo, Monashee, Selkirk and Purcell Mountains. The Rocky Mountain Trench separates these ranges from the Rocky Mountains, which run along the B.C./Alberta border in the south, and north to the Yukon border. The Rocky Mountains are high and spectacular. Visitors sometimes refer to all the western mountains as the Rockies.

The fifth region, the *Northeast Lowland* in the top corner of the province has both hilly and flat terrain. The southern Peace River area is good land for crops and cattle. The north corner contains swampy, sparse, spruce forests.

Internet Links: Maps at **Canada Info Link** and Geography Quizzes at **Fun Trivia**. Easylinks at **donnaward.net**

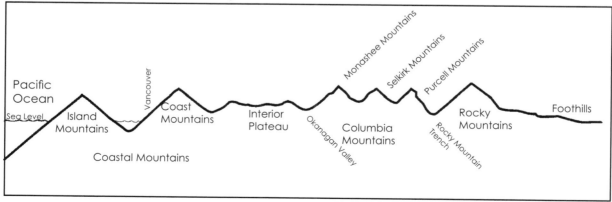

Why is it incorrect to refer to the Western Mountains as The Rocky Mountains?

Lesson 11~Geography

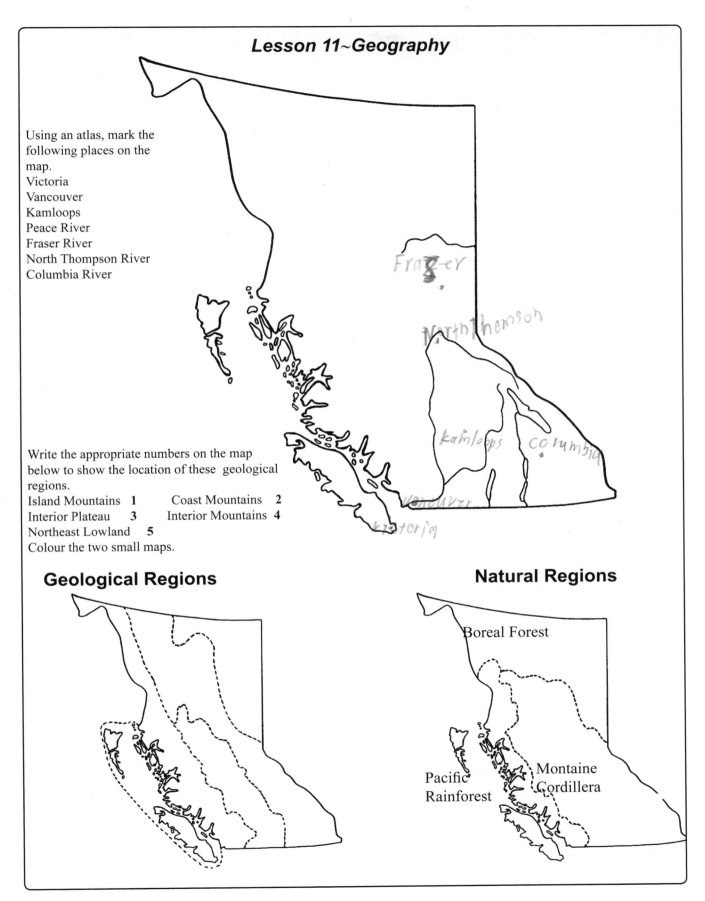

Using an atlas, mark the following places on the map.

Victoria
Vancouver
Kamloops
Peace River
Fraser River
North Thompson River
Columbia River

Write the appropriate numbers on the map below to show the location of these geological regions.

Island Mountains **1**   Coast Mountains **2**
Interior Plateau   **3**   Interior Mountains **4**
Northeast Lowland   **5**
Colour the two small maps.

Geological Regions

Natural Regions

Boreal Forest

Pacific Rainforest

Montaine Cordillera

The sweet smell of pine, blazing red maples, crunching leaves, flitting birds—Canadians love their forests! Forests conjure up memories of vacations, afternoon walks, and discovery. It's no wonder; almost half of our total land area is covered in forests.

Canada is in first place as a world exporter of forest products. More goods come from the forest industry than fish, farm, and mineral products put together. One of every 10 Canadians works in some area of the forest industry.

Logging

Logging involves harvesting the trees, transporting the wood to mill sites, and reforestation. Timber is a renewable resource when proper care is taken. In the past, forests were cut with little thought given to the development of new trees. Now, government regulations require logging companies to replant and plan ahead so that forests are available for future generations.

Though logging restrictions are more stringent than in the past, many environmentalists are not satisfied. In British Columbia, where mature trees can be 200 to 1,000 years old, environmentalists have clashed with foresters in an effort to save "old-growth" forests. Both the effect on the environment and the economy are important considerations in this dispute.

Lumberjack or Logger?

In the 1800's foresters of the east became known as lumberjacks. That term died out and they are now called loggers. In B.C., they have always been called loggers.

Was Paul Bunyan a real person?

Did you know that the tall tales of lumberjack Paul Bunyan were likely based on a logger from Ottawa? Born in Montreal, Joe Montferrand became the amateur boxing champion of Quebec. As a rafting foreman on the Ottawa River, he became known as one who ran faster, jumped higher and hit harder than anyone else. When he battled 10 Irishmen on a bridge, the story was retold over and over until it was said that he fought 150 men. These legends were repeated in shanty camps across the nation and each tale became "taller" as it was repeated.

Wood Processing

Wood processing includes all the steps from cutting lumber in the sawmill to the production of wood products which are available on store shelves. In *primary* wood processing, sawmills prepare the lumber for use in construction and to sell to manufacturers. In the *secondary* industries, the manufacturers produce items such as sports equipment, furniture, flooring, matches, doors, and so on. Look around your room and count how many products you can see that are processed from wood.

Pulp and Paper

The biggest component of the forest industry is pulp and paper. Canada supplies one third of the world's newsprint for newspapers and more than half of all the newspaper used in the United States. We also export wood pulp, which is the prepared fiber used to make paper. Black spruce, abundant in the Boreal Forest and too small to be sawn into lumber, has dense long fibers excellently suited for making paper.

Danger to our Forest Resources

Forests are threatened not only by logging, but also by insects, which destroy large tracts of forest each year. In eastern Canada, the spruce budworm is the most devastating pest, eating the buds and needles of softwood conifers. In B.C., the pine bark beetle destroys many large pines. Chemical pest killers (pesticides) can cause damage to the environment and other wildlife, therefore, scientists continue to look for new ways to fight these bugs.

Canadians are more passionate about their specific region than they are about their country. The diversity across our land in both geography and culture, and the vast distances that separate us, keep us in love with our own little piece of land more than the whole.

Another naturally occurring threat is the forest fire. Forests damaged in remote areas have been ignited by lightning and are left to burn themselves out. Many of the fires close to human activities are started by careless people.

In the past, all forest fires were thought to be a devastating hazard which should be eliminated completely. Now, forest managers realize fires are not just destructive, but can be productive, opening the way for new, healthier growth. Fires clear stands of old wood that can choke out young trees. The ash left in the soil provides nutrients for new growth. Two trees, the black spruce and the lodgepole pine, actually need fire to release the seeds from the cones. Forest firefighters concentrate on protecting homes, recreational areas, and logging zones, leaving distant fires to die out on their own.

The forests, one of Canada's most extensive renewable resources, provide beauty, shelter, jobs, and innumerable products for our homes. Forests are not only ours to enjoy but to look after as well.

If you planned to bicycle across Canada, would it be better to go from west to east or from east to west?

USA cyclist Mandy Joselin pedalled 100 km. each day for 75 days, travelling from Vancouver to St. John's. She advised that since prevailing winds across the country blow from the northwest, by starting in the west you will have advantageous winds 75% of the way.

The people of Canada are generally private, polite, and conservative. Rather than elevate themselves or their heroes, they tend to minimize achievements and stick to realities.

Lesson 12~Forestry

1. As an exporter of forestry products, in what place does Canada rank in the world?

    a) third place   b) first place   c) fifth place   d) tenth place

2. Is timber a renewable product or a non-renewable product? Explain why.

    A Tree has seeds on it to groeh fresh trees

3. In British Columbia environmentalists have clashed with the forest industry over what issue?

    To sqve old growth forest

4. Match the process or product to the appropriate area of the forest industry.

    Logging   furniture
                               newsprint
                               replanting trees
    Wood Processing   construction lumber
                               wood pulp
    Pulp and Paper   harvesting trees
                               baseball bats

5. What two insects are very destructive to Canada's forests?

    spruce bud werm, pine bark beetle

6. Name two reasons why forest fires can be good for a forest.

    They burn old stumps
    so they can release thier cones

Population

B.C.:   3,907,738
Victoria: 335,000 (provincial capital)
Vancouver: 2,208,300

B.C. Hazards - Earthquakes

B.C. is both spectacular and hazardous. The province lies in a high risk earthquake zone. In 1946, an earthquake on Vancouver Island caused the chimneys of a school to collapse into the classrooms. Fortunately, it was Sunday and no children were in the building. In 1964, an earthquake in Alaska caused a tidal wave 7 metres high. The coastal city of Port Alberni was hit the hardest as cars and houses were thrown into the air and logs were slammed through buildings. Thankfully, the people had been evacuated and no one was harmed.

Storms

B.C.'s rocky coastline, combined with ferocious storms, have caused many shipwrecks throughout history. About 2000 vessels each year get into trouble in B.C. waters, keeping the Canadian coastguard busy, and appreciated.

Avalanches

The highways department in B.C. has a special branch just to look after avalanche danger on the roads. Around 1600 avalanches occur each year near highways and the specialists often use explosives to make the snow fall before it can become a serious threat. At least one person per year dies in an avalanche, usually while engaged in sports like snowmobiling or skiing.

History Highlights

	Natives of North Pacific Coast, and Plateau live in B.C.
1778	James Cook lands at Nootka Sound, Vancouver Island
1793	Alexander Mackenzie reaches Pacific Ocean by land.
1794	George Vancouver maps coast
1857	Gold discovered in Fraser Valley
1858	British Columbia established as a colony
1871	B.C. joins Confederation with the promise of a railway link
1885	Railway finished

Alex MacKenzie from Canada by land 22d July 1793

When the Canadian flag was first officially flown, was there a prayer?

On Parliament Hill, February 15, 1965, Canadians proudly watched the first official unfurling of the National Flag of Canada. Governor General Georges P. Vanier recited the following prayer:
"Bless, O Merciful Father, this Flag and grant that this banner of our nationhood may proudly fly over a people devoted to the pursuit of righteousness, justice, and unity; whose faith and hopes are grounded in Thee, who art the King of Kings and the Lord of Lords."

Internet Links: See footage of Avalanche control explosives at Roger's Pass on **CBC archives**. Easylinks at **donnaward.net**

Colour the population bar graph.
See library books on B.C. (adult & children's library section 917.11).
Also: Mark Zuehlke, *Fun B.C. Facts for Kids*. (1996).

ALBERTA THE PRINCESS PROVINCE

My hair's mostly wind, my eyes filled with grit
My skin's white then brown, my lips chapped and split
I've lain on the prairie and heard grasses sigh
I've stared at the vast open bowl of the sky
I've seen all the castles and faces in clouds
My home is the prairie and for that I am proud . . .

And the prairie continues to live in my heart
It's much more than memories that tell me apart
It's the wind and the sun, the cold and the snow
Only things that a child of the prairie will know.

Dave Bouchard. *Prairie Born.*
(Victoria: Orca Book Pub., 1997).

Alberta was named after Princess Louise Caroline Alberta, who was the fourth daughter of Queen Victoria and also the wife of one of Canada's Governor Generals. Lake Louise, in Banff National Park, and Caroline, the small hometown of world figure skating champion, Kurt Browning, were also named in her honour.

Great Horned Owl

A solitary bird, the Great Horned Owl is a merciless hunter who moves out at dusk looking for rabbits, squirrels, and even farm chickens or ducks. This hunter takes on prey larger than any other owl would tackle and has been known to kill several turkeys in a night. It may feast on the heads only and leave the rest of the prey for scavengers. The deep-toned *to-whoo-hoo-hoo, to-whoo-hoo,* all on the same note, the familiar owl sound, is the call of the Great Horned Owl.

> What could be more beautiful than the way the sky stretches away to the horizon - gives a man room to breathe.
> John G. Diefenbaker
> Canadian Prime Minister

Wild Rose

The pink Wild Rose, with its bright yellow centre, grows along roadside and in prairie meadows.

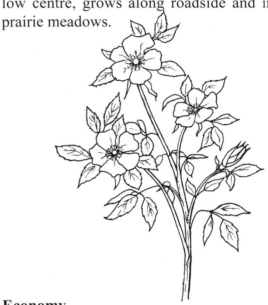

Economy

Alberta was chiefly a farming area until the 1947 discovery of oil changed the economy. Many Albertans have prospered as the province has become the number one oil producer in Canada. Alberta also possesses rich farmland where more beef cattle are raised than in any other province. Wheat is still the most important crop.

Internet Links: Try the Great Horned Owl Maze and view photos at **Kid Zone**. Listen to the sound of the owl at **Cornell Lab of Ornithology.** Easylinks at **donnaward.**

Lesson 14~Symbols

Research and appropriately colour each symbol.

Wild Rose

Great Horned Owl

Symbols of the Shield
(give the meanings of the symbols on the shield)

Cross of St. George: _symboliz̄es Albertas_
historic association with Greatbritian

Landscape: _stand for canadian_
Rockies.

Grain: _Albertas chief crop._
_____

Shield

ALBERTA

While B.C. has some of the most spectacular scenery, Alberta offers the most diverse, from huge mountains to flat prairie. The province contains part of the *Western Cordillera Region*, the *Interior Plain,* and the *Canadian Shield.*

Along the B.C./Alberta border, the Rocky Mountains of the *Western Cordillera* soar in awesome beauty, surrounding tourist towns like Banff and Jasper. Beyond the mountains, the foothills extend east toward the Plains.

The majority of Alberta is level *Interior Plains.* The vegetation of the Plains varies from north to south. In the far north the tree-less tundra is called the Taiga Plains. South of this, the Boreal Forest Plain spreads its green covering of spruce and pine. The conifers become sparse in the transitional Aspen Parkland Plain where birch and aspen trees mix with grass and farmland. From the Parkland south to the USA border, the Prairies, once hectares of grassland, now ripple with fields of grain. Trees are sparsely scattered across the landscape. Most people think of the Prairies as flat, having seen such terrain along the trans-Canada highway in the south. There are, however, a lot of areas with rolling hills.

In the far southeast corner, the *Hills* rise to meet the Saskatchewan/Alberta border, and in the northeast corner a small portion of the *Canadian Shield* juts into Alberta.

The *Western Corillera* in this province creates unusual weather because it blocks the moist air from the Pacific Ocean. As the air rises to pass over the mountains, much of the moisture falls on the western slopes before it reaches Alberta. The air warms as it flows down onto the Plains, producing dry winds and even desert-like areas.

The warm air also produces some bizarre weather changes called "chinooks." Occurring in winter and spring, chinooks can warm the temperature up to 25 °C in an hour, and Albertans don shorts and T-shirts to enjoy the short relapse from the frosty winter.

All kinds of adventures are available for Canadians or visitors enjoying Alberta's unique and varied landscape.

How do you refer to residents of various towns or cities?	Try naming the residents of these places:	
		Hope-ite (4)
1. If the name ends in -*a*, or -*ia*, add -*n*		Jasperite (5)
Ottawan, Orillian	Aklavik (YK)	Reginan (1)
2. If the name ends in -*y*, change the *y* to *i*, add -*an* and shift the stress	Labrador City (NFLD)	Brandonian (3)
Calgarian	Fredericton (NB)	Sudburian (2)
3. If the name ends in -*on* or -*outh*, usually add -*ian*	Charlottetown (PEI)	Alman (1)
Edmontonian, Dartmouthian	Truro (NS)	Truroite (4)
4. If the name ends in a vowel other than -*a*, add -*ite*, sometimes with a hyphen, sometimes	Alma (QC)	Charlottetowner (5)
without.	Sudbury (ON)	Frederictonian (3)
Nanaimoite, Portage la Prairie-ite	Brandon (MB)	Labrador Citian (2)
5. If the name ends with a consonant, in some cases add -*er*, in other cases add -*ite*.	Regina (SK)	Aklaviker (5)
Quebecer, Murray Harbourite	Jasper (AB)	Answers Rule#
	Hope (BC)	

Internet Links: Alberta relief map at **Canada Info Link.** Alberta Quizzes at **Fun Trivia.** Easylink at **donnaward.net**

Lesson 15~Geography

Write the appropriate numbers on the map below to show the location of these geological regions.

Western Cordillera	**1**	Plains	**2**
Canadian Shield	**3**	Hills	**4**

Colour the two small maps.

Using an atlas, mark the following places on the map below.

Peace River (city)	Peace River
Edmonton	Athabasca River
Calgary	North Saskatchewan River
Medicine Hat	Red Deer River
Banff	Bow River
Jasper	

Geological Regions

Natural Regions

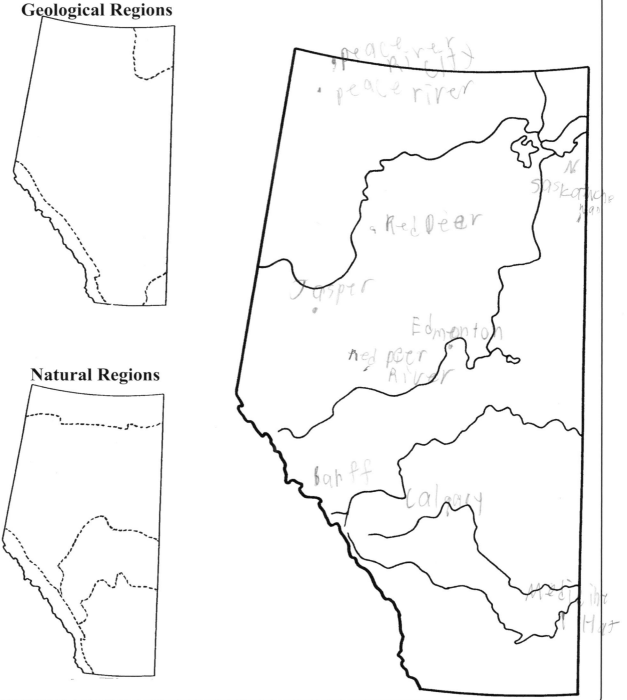

The rosy chill bites your cheeks as you trudge home through the snow. Dusk comes early, but the cheery light in your window beckons and you burst through the door shaking snow off your coat. The aroma of chicken roasting welcomes you, as your Mom plugs in the kettle for hot chocolate. Do you love those cold winter nights when you are snug and warm in your cosy home?

The lighting, heating, and cooking you experience all require some kind of energy. Canada is one of the world's highest energy users. Why?

1) Canada is cold for over six months of the year and people have to heat their homes and work places. Of the total energy used in a year, families use 19% in their homes, and businesses use 15% to heat and light their buildings.

2) Canada's huge size means that goods and people must travel long distances. Transportation requires 30% of Canada's energy.

3) Canada's factories, mills, and refineries need a great deal of energy to operate; 31% of the Canadian total.

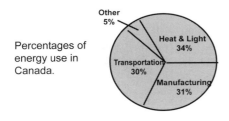

Percentages of energy use in Canada.

Other 5%
Heat & Light 34%
Transportation 30%
Manufacturing 31%

Canadians have a number of choices regarding the kind of energy they will use. Some forms are *renewable* such as falling water, which can be converted to electricity. Other sources of energy, like oil or coal, are replaced so slowly by nature that they are considered *non-renewable*. Once they are used, they can not be replaced.

A soot-coated truck pulled up to our house. Covered in grime, the driver grimaced as he hauled the heavy sack onto his back and trudged across the snow. Black dust left a dirty trail behind him. I heard the rumble as the coal poured in through the basement window into the bin below.

I watched from the kitchen as he went back for another load. He waved and smiled at me, showing glistening white teeth and the glowing whites of his eyes against his soot blackened face. After many such trips, our coal bin was full.

Every night Father shovelled coal into the furnace and piled it up against the burning embers. By morning however, the fire would be low and the house so cold! Very early, Father was down stoking the furnace. Mom would bring our underwear and stockings to put on under the warm covers. We listened for the crackling of the radiator pipes as the house slowly warmed up. That was in the days when we heated our homes with coal.

Young childhood memories of the 1930's.

Sometimes in a piece of coal the imprint of a leaf can be seen. This occurs because coal is made from fossils of plant life which, through pressure, became soft, black rock. Coal burns efficiently to create energy. It used to be the predominant fuel for heating homes, but now its chief use is in manufacturing. Saskatchewan, Alberta, and B.C. contain Canada's largest deposits of coal. Coal is also mined in Nova Scotia and New Brunswick.

If you saw black stuff oozing out of the ground in your back yard, what would you think? You might shout something like, "black gold!" and hope you had struck it rich. In Canada, oil was first discovered bubbling to the surface near the Ontario towns of Oil Springs and Petrolia.

The word *petroleum* comes from two Latin words for *rock* and *oil*, for it was found seeping up through cracks in rocks. Oilmen today call the substance *crude oil*.

> Petroleum refers to both crude oil and natural gas, although it is sometimes used to mean oil only.

Although no one knows for sure how oil was formed, most scientists believe that long ago ancient plants and sea animals died and became buried under layers of mud in the bottom of lakes. As sediment piled up its weight pressed the mud into layers of rock. The plant and animal remains were changed by decay into a liquid and gas state. The liquid oil gathered in tiny holes in the rock. The gas, known as *natural gas,* filled the cavities above the oil.

Large amounts of oil have been found in places known in Canada as the sedimentary basins: areas which were large lakes at one time. Usually, the oil and gas is held deep under the rock and wells have to be drilled to gain access to the oil.

In the early years, drillers considered natural gas a nuisance. Since it floated above the oil, it had to be burned off to access the oil. Then men discovered that gas was an excellent home heating fuel: both less expensive and cleaner burning. Now natural gas has replaced oil in many areas.

The discovery of oil in Alberta triggered extensive oil exploration across Canada. As well as Alberta, oil is mined in B.C. and Saskatchewan. Offshore deposits were found on the continental shelf off the coast of Newfoundland and Nova Scotia. The largest offshore development, the Hibernia oil field near Newfoundland, is expected to produce oil for twenty years. Alberta, however, remains the Canadian leader for petroleum products.

Both oil and gas can be transported across the country and even into the United States in an economical way. Extensive pipelines connect Alberta oil fields to eastern Canada, as well as to British Columbia and the USA

How is your home heated? How does your hot water heat: by electricity or natural gas? What are the different energy fuels that your family uses? While Canadians have a wealth of energy sources, we still need to be good stewards of our resources and not waste them. Discuss with your family how you can conserve energy in your home.

Was Jerry Potts a bad guy or good guy?

Half Native, half Scottish, Potts was a wrangler, hunter, guide and fur trader in Montana and Alberta. When Natives of Alberta needed protection from USA whiskey traders, Potts was hired to guide the North-West Mounted Police to Fort Whoop-up. The little man with drooping shoulders and a chin of whiskers was the most talented scout ever associated with the Mounted Police. Famous officer, Sam Steele, described Potts' scouts as the best-trained ever seen. Upon his death in 1896, Jerry Potts was buried with full military honours.

1. Name three reasons why Canada is a country which uses a lot of energy.

   It is cold over six months of the year.

   Canada's huge size.

   canada's factories, mills, and refineries,

2. Name two non-renewable forms of energy.

   oil, coal

3. At one time most homes in Canada were heated by coal. Where is coal most often used now? Name three provinces where coal is mined.

   manufactoring

   Saskatchewan, Alberta, B.C.

4. From what two words was the term *petroleum* taken, and why? What is the term for petroleum today?

   oil, rock, crude oil

5. Name two reasons why natural gas is a good home heating fuel.

   less expensive, cleaner burning

7. What two provinces contain offshore oil deposits?

   Newfoundland, Nova scotia

8. How is your home heated?

   wood

Population

Alberta:　　2,974,806
Edmonton:　1,016,000 (provincial capital)
Calgary:　　1,060,300

Cowboys of the Range

Choking on the dust, the young cowhand pulled his bandana over his nose. "Get along little dogie," he yelled at a faltering calf as it stumbled at the back of the herd. Could this little one make the hundred kilometers yet to go on the cattle drive from Montana to Alberta?

Leading the drive, the trail boss rode at the front while experienced cowhands flanked each side, watchful for strays or spooked cows. New cowhands rode in the rear, following the dust of the herd

This herd was being bought by an Alberta rancher who knew there was money to be made in beef. The government had to feed the North-West Mounted Police and the Natives as the buffalo was gone.

With acres of free grazing land, ranchers branded their cattle and then let them roam loose until roundup time.

The spring roundup, a cooperative effort between all the ranchers, was very gruelling. Each chuckwagon, driven by a cook, supplied meals for about 12 cowhands. Starting in southern Alberta, groups worked different areas rounding up all the cattle on the range and the river valleys, driving them towards specified areas. Cattle were separated according to their brands. The owners then counted them, branded new calves, and picked

History Highlights

Natives of the Plains and Natives of the Subarctic dwell on land

1754　Fur Traders begin coming to trade with the First Nations & build trading posts

1873　American wolf hunters massacre Assiniboine Natives at Cypress Hills

1874　North-West Mounted Police come to protect First Nations people

1883　Railway completed to Calgary Arrival of immigrant settlers

Alberta becomes a province

1905

out steers for the beef market. The fall roundup was more local and usually just for the purpose of acquiring more beef to sell.

As the railway snaked its way across the plains, ranchers were both glad but worried. On the one hand, the railway made transporting cattle to markets much easier. However, it also brought settlers who tilled the valuable grazing land and blocked cattle routes with their fences.

The sale of grazing lands for agriculture was the end of large ranches on the plains, but Stetson hats, cowboy boots, and rodeos keep alive the memory of the golden days of ranching in Alberta.

Colour the population bar graph.
See library books on Alberta (adult & children's library section 917.11, 917.12).
Also: Elaine Wheaton, *But It's a Dry Cold.* (1998)

SASKATCHEWAN CANADA'S BREAD BASKET

The drama of this landscape is in the sky, pouring with light and always moving . . . . It is a long way from characterless; "overpowering" would be a better word. For over the segmented circle of earth is domed the biggest sky anywhere, which on days like this sheds down on range and wheat and summer fallow a light to set a painter wild, a light pure, glareless, and transparent. The horizon a dozen miles away is as clean a line as the nearest fence.

Wallace Stegner. *Wolf Willow.*
(New York: Viking Press, 1955).

The two branches of the Saskatchewan River—the North Saskatchewan and the South Saskatchewan—flow out of Alberta, join near the city of Prince Albert, and drain into Lake Winnipeg in Manitoba. An important water route for aboriginals and fur traders, both branches of the river carried people and goods across the province to the foothills of the Rockies. The Cree called it *Kisiskatchewani Sipe,* meaning "swift-flowing" river and from this Indian term the province took its name.

Sharp-Tailed Grouse

A true prairie lover, the Sharp-tailed Grouse is one of the best known game birds, prized for its tender meat. Famous for the spring courting dance, the male first distends sacs at his neck, then ruffs up his feathers, and finally beats the ground in a thumping hop. Another male may rush in and the crazy birds twist, stamp, and jump over each other in an effort to impress a mate. After pairing, the female is left to nest in the grass and tend the brood alone. Sharp-tailed Grouse scavenge the ground for insects, seeds, and berries. In winter, the birds move into sheltered ravines and treed areas where they roost in the branches.

Western Red Lily

The Western Red Lily, with its crimson-orange a bold contrast to the prairie hues, is found in damp meadows and marshy glens.

Economy

Saskatchewan's greatest resource is its farmland, greater in area than farmland in any other province. The most important crop, wheat, earns the province its nickname as the "bread basket" of Canada. Saskatchewan is a major producer of petroleum products. Uranium and potash are also valuable mining resources.

Is the North-West Mounted Police the same as the Royal Canadian Mounted Police?

The North-West Mounted Police (NWMP) protected the west and north. The Dominion Police brought law to the east. In 1920, the forces merged to become the Royal Canadian Mounted Police (RCMP). Headquarters was moved from Regina to Ottawa. The RCMP training college is still in Regina.

What was Regina's earlier name?

The present day capital of Saskatchewan was once called "Wascana," which means "Pile of Bones." This was considered an unsuitable name, therefore, in 1882, the city was renamed Regina in honour of Queen Victoria.

Internet Links: Listen to the sound of the Sharp-Tailed Grouse at **Cornell Lab of Ornithology**. Easylinks at **donnaward.net**

Lesson 18~Symbols

Research and appropriately colour each symbol.

Western Red Lily

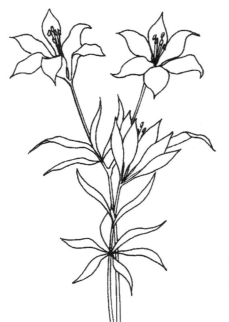

Sharp-tailed Grouse

Symbols of the Shield
(give the meanings of the symbols on the shield)

Shield

Red Lion: _british crown_

_____

Wheat Sheaves: _a resource of the_

province.

SASKATCHEWAN

Visitors to the Plains of Saskatchewan may interpret the uninterrupted fields of farmland as boring, but residents love the land like a sailor loves the sea: the endless view from horizon to horizon, glorious sunsets, violent storms, and the vast fields of rippling grain. The *Interior Plains* are the most well-known and largest region in Saskatchewan geography. The other region is the *Canadian Shield* in the north.

The *Plains* stretch in a series of rolling hills, flat lands, and deep river valleys. The southwest corner of Saskatchewan contains the *Hills* regions, where the unusual Great Sand Hills, the barren Big Muddy Badlands, and the Cypress Hills stretch into Alberta. Saskatchewan's northeast corner is dominated by the *Canadian Shield* region.

Like Alberta, the natural vegetation of the Plains is *Prairie* in the south, and then *Aspen Parkland* where birch, aspen, farmland, and grassland combine to meet the northern Boreal Forest.

In the *Canadian Shield*, the *Boreal Forest* mixes with numerous lakes, bogs, and rocky outcrops. The most northerly part of the province is treeless, an area called the *Taiga Shield.*

All dwellers of the prairie experience the constant wind that stings and bites in winter, and cools the hot land in summer. Within minutes, the winds can blow a storm or tornado from a once sunny sky. Summer hail storms can damage crops and winter snow storms make walking from the house to the barn a dangerous hazard. It is easy to get lost in a blowing white-out. Temperature extremes in summer and winter are all part of the adventure of living on the prairies.

Internet Links: Ecoregions map of Saskatchewan at **Virtual Saskatchewan Ecoregions** (scroll down). Quizzes at **Fun Trivia**. Easylinks at **donnaward.net**

What is it about weather that fascinates people?. . .Our preoccupation - some might call it an obsession - with the weather must be perplexing to folk from milder climates who have to suffer through the boredom of consistent temperatures and conditions. (What do they talk about?) But despite our frequent grumbling, we're proud of our weather - or rather, we're proud of our ability to endure anything nature dishes out. We routinely survive the extremes of almost every type of weather imaginable.

The field of our dreams is flooded and frozen and has a net at either end.
Joey Slinger
Canadian columnist

[1] Elaine Wheaton. *But It's a Dry Cold.* (Calgary: Fifth House Pub., 1998), p. 1.

Lesson 19~Geography

Write the appropriate numbers on the map below to show the location of these geological regions.

Plains   **1**   Canadian Shield   **2**
Hills   **3**
Colour the two small maps.

Using an atlas, mark the following places on the map below.

Regina	South Saskatchewan River
Saskatoon	North Saskatchewan River
Moose Jaw	Qu'Appelle River
Uranium City	Lake Athabasca
Lloydminster	Lake Diefenbaker

Geological Regions

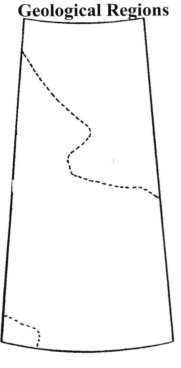

Natural Regions

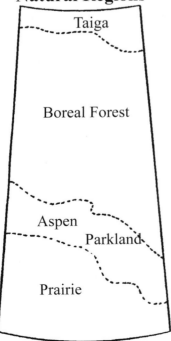

Taiga

Boreal Forest

Aspen

Parkland

Prairie

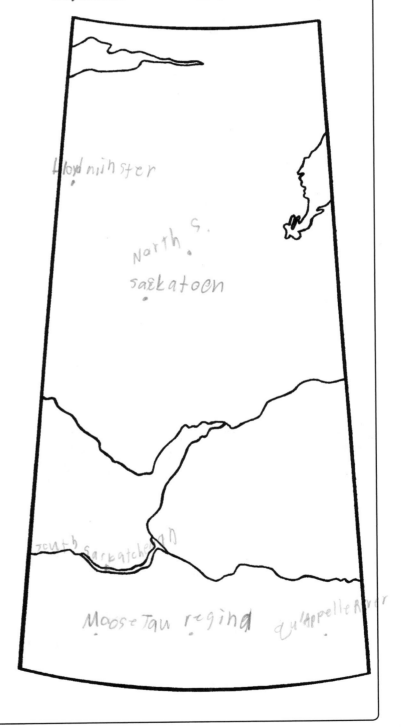

In settlement days, immigrants flocked to Canada with the promise of good farmland. Most of the people were farmers. Today, however, only 3 percent of Canadians farm, yet enough food is produced to feed our population as well as to export to other nations. Larger farms and specialized equipment make this possible.

Only a small amount of Canada's vast land is productive for farming. Adequate rain, fertile soil, level land, and warm days are the key ingredients for good agricultural land. Coastal B.C., for instance, has lots of rain but only a small area of level land. Southern Alberta has level land and warm summer days, but low precipitation. Saskatchewan's farmland meets all the key ingredients and has over one-third of Canada's productive farmland.

If you bought a farm, how would you decide what to plant? The length of the growing season is one key factor. There have to be enough days over 5.6°C for crops to mature. Wheat, for example, takes 100 days to ripen, while corn requires 150 days.

Southern Ontario, with its longer growing season, is known for its corn production, while Saskatchewan is famous for vast wheat crops.

You may hear a farmer describe the size of his farm in acres. This measure was used in the past, but now the size of farms in Canada is calculated in hectares (ha). There are about 2.5 acres in a hectare. There are 100 hectares in a square kilometre.

GOOD AGRICULTURAL LAND BY PROVINCE	
Province	% of Total Farmland
Saskatchewan	35.4
Alberta	23.3
Ontario	15.8
Manitoba	11.2
Quebec	4.8
British Columbia	3.2
New Brunswick	2.9
Nova Scotia	2.5
PEI	0.9
Newfoundland*	0.0
Canada	100.0

*Newfoundland has less than one percent of the farmland of Canada's total area.[1]

The kinds of farms depend on the quality of farmland and the climate. The four main types are: *field crops, livestock, fruit and vegetable,* and *mixed farming.* Mixed farming is a mixture of crops and livestock.

[1] Adapted from *This Land of Ours.* Krueger, Ralph (Toronto: Harcourt Brace Jovanovich Canada Inc. 1991), p. 270.

The average Saskatchewan *field crops* farm is 420 hectares which is huge compared to a 50 hectare vegetable farm in Ontario. Specialized tractors and combines make wheat farming expensive to set up and run. Prairie farmers grow other grain crops such as oats, barley, and rye along with oil seeds like canola and sunflowers which are used to make cooking oil. Grain farmers work hard planting in spring and harvesting in fall. Winter is a low activity season.

Livestock farming includes beef cattle, dairy cattle, pigs, poultry, and other speciality animals. The highest percentage of beef cattle is raised in the west where dry grassland is not suitable for grains. Cattle ranchers need less machinery but more land for cattle to graze. The average size of a cattle ranch is 640 ha. Cattle are either sold in the fall or fed on grain and hay until spring.

Dairy farms are predominant in Quebec and Ontario. Milking and refrigeration equipment make initial costs of starting a dairy farm the highest of all. Farmers grow hay and grain for winter feed. Dairy farms average about 132 ha. in size. There is no slow season, for cattle have to be fed and milked every day of the year!

Vegetable farms need a long growing season and to be close in distance to city markets, as vegetables are damaged easily in transportation. It takes a lot of labour and specialized equipment for the planting and harvesting of vegetables. Generally, these farms are about 55 hectares in size. The work is heavy from the start of spring planting to the last of fall harvesting. Tender *fruit farms* produce grapes, peaches, pears, cherries, plums, and apples. Only two areas in Canada are suitable for a high yield of commercial fruits, the Niagara fruit belt in Ontario and the Okanagan Valley in British Columbia. Because of the intensive labour of trimming, spraying, and harvesting, the farms are only about 30 hectares in size. Fruit farming profits are not high and many farmers sell fertile farmland for city expansion. What do you think about this?

In Saskatchewan, many family farms have been bought and combined with other farms to create large tracts of land now manageable with modern farming machinery. The result, however, is many empty farm houses left to decay.

There have certainly been a lot of changes from early farming to farming in Canada

In some parts of the prairies. . . . crumbling houses outnumber the flourishing homes. . . . By now the grandchildren of the men and women who broke the land and built the little towns are often ensconced in the suburbs of Regina or Vancouver, and to the great majority of them these peeling, leaning houses are nothing more than relics of the hard passage to a safe prosperity. But depopulation gives the country a sombre, beaten look . . . . If the pioneers could have glimpsed the state of comfort that most of their descendants enjoy, no doubt they would have been delighted. Had they also seen the fate of their homes, land and communities, many would have felt dismay.[1]

Internet Links: Go to **CBC Archives**/Disasters and Tragedies/Extreme Weather to learn the history of drought in the prairies. Easylinks at **donnaward.net**

[1] Mark Abley. *Beyond Forget, Rediscovering the Prairies.* (Toronto: Douglas & McIntyre, 1986), p. 8.

Lesson 20~Farming

1. What is the percentage of Canadians who farm today? What makes it possible for so few to grow all the food Canadians need?

3% large farms and spezilied equipment.

2. What four ingredients result in good farmland?

adequate rain, fertile soil, level land, and warm days.

3. Name the four main kinds of farms.

field crops, livestock, fruit and vegetable

4. Match a province to a type of farming important to that province. Although one province may have various kinds of farms, pick the one which most closely matches.

Alberta   Fruit
Saskatchewan   Livestock - beef
Quebec   Field Crops
Prince Edward Island   Vegetables
British Columbia   Livestock - dairy

5. Using the information on page 47, colour the bar graph showing the percentage of Canada's total farmland in each province.

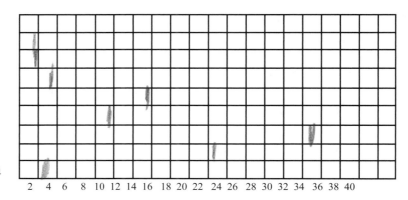

PEI
Nova Scotia
New Brunswick
Quebec
Ontario
Manitoba
Saskatchewan
Alberta
British Columbia
Percentage of Total   2 4 6 8 10 12 14 16 18 20 22 24 26 28 30 32 34 36 38 40

Population

Saskatchewan: 978,933
Regina: 199,000 (provincial capital)
Saskatoon: 236,056

Saskatchewan Highlights

Agriculture is the lifeblood of Saskatchewan. Many factors affect the success of crops, but none so dramatically as the weather. Extreme variations can wipe out an entire year's earnings. In the 1930s, severe drought brought on disaster from which many farmers never recovered. They had to leave their farms and move north where the rain was more reliable, or move out of the province.

Farmers today watch the weather carefully. Hail, frost, or rain can damage or destroy crops. With each new spring comes the hope of a bumper harvest, therefore, in bad times farmers shrug and say, "Wait until next year."

The Dust Bowl

In the 1930's, a decade of drought in the prairies, which included dust storms and crop failures, brought disaster and hardship to many Canadians. Top soil was blown from the fields to pile up against fences, buildings, and ditches. With the crash of the stock market in 1929 and the drought in the west, thousands were out of work. Farms were abandoned. Many families packed what they could, closed the doors on their farmhouses and headed east. It was a time of bread lines, hobos, and despair, known as the Great Depression. Improved conditions came only after World War II.

History Highlights

	Natives of the Plains and Subarctic Hunters occupy the land.
1774	Samuel Hearne initiates fur trade and building of Cumberland House (first permanent European settlement)
1874	North-West Mounted Police come to enforce law in the west
1882	Canadian Pacific Railway reaches Regina
1885	Louis Riel & forces start the North-West Rebellion but are defeated
1905	Saskatchewan becomes a province

What happened to the name Dominion of Canada?

In 1866, when the Fathers of Confederation were deciding on a name for our country, Sir Leonard Tilley suggested the term *Dominion.* That morning he had read from the Bible, Psalm 72:8, "He shall have dominion also from sea to sea." The men agreed and the country officially became "The Dominion of Canada." Canada's motto, "from sea to sea," also came from this Bible passage.

In the past few decades, Liberal governments began to drop the term 'Dominion' from government documents. The term 'Canada' or 'Government of Canada' soon replaced the original name.

This move has made many people unhappy. In 1970, Donald Creighton, famed historian at the University of Toronto, complained that the government just quietly dropped the word 'Dominion' without making any official statement or policy.

Colour the population bar graph.
See library books on Saskatchewan (adult & children's library section 917.12).
Also: William Kurelek, *A Prairie Boy's Winter* (1973), William Kurelek, *A Prairie Boy's Summer (1970).*
David Bouchard, *Prairie Born* (1997), David Bouchard, *If You're Not From the Prairie* (1993).

49

MANITOBA THE KEYSTONE PROVINCE

If you're not from the prairie,
You've not heard the grass,
You've never heard grass.
In strong summer winds, the grains and grass bend
And sway to a dance that seems never to end.
It whispers its secrets - they tell of this land
And the rhythm of life played by nature's own hand.
If you're not from the prairie,
You've never heard grass.

David Bouchard. *If You're Not From the Prairie.*
(Vancouver: Raincoast Books, 1993).

A keystone is the stone at the top of an arch which holds all other stones in place. Similarly, Manitoba is central in Canada, the doorway to the west, and the connection to the east. Thus it has been nicknamed the "Keystone Province."

When the waves lapped the rocky shore at the narrows of Lake Manitoba, it sounded like someone whispering. In heavy winds, it sounded like the beat of a drum. The Native people said it was Manito, their Great Spirit speaking. When the area joined Canada in 1870, Louis Riel suggested the name Manitoba, after the Cree words for Great Spirit and Narrows.

Great Gray Owl

The world's largest owl, the Great Gray Owl, is rarely seen, keeping to dense woods of the far north. It measures 90 cm long with a wing span up to 150 cm. (Measure that with a meter stick. You'll be amazed!) So sharp is this owl's hearing, that it can dive through deep snow and accurately strike a mouse it has heard but not seen. Its legs are heavily feathered to help it stay warm in the northern winters. The Great Gray Owl ranges as far north as the tree line.

Prairie Crocus

After a long, cold winter, there is nothing more welcome than a sure sign of spring. The Prairie Crocus, in its various purples, peeps through the last snow to promise the coming of warm days. Its coating of fine hair protects it from sudden weather changes.

Economics

Agriculture has always been one of Manitoba's strongest industries where farmland is some of the most fertile in Canada. Wheat, canola, sunflower seeds, rye, and oats are grown. The manufacturing sector employs a lot of people, especially in Winnipeg.

The Peaceable Nation

Canada has been called "The Peaceable Kingdom." It was the first country, having been a colony of the Old World, to gain independence without violent revolution. Canada has never started a war. Canada has been a part of every major peacekeeping operation since the conception of the United Nations which was organized to facilitate world peace.

What was the first "chain store" system?

The Hudson's Bay Company was the first "chain store" system in the world. It traded and sold all kinds of goods to Natives and settlers.

Internet Links: Listen to the sound of the Great Gray Owl at **Cornell Lab of Ornithology**. Manitoba quizzes at **Fun Trivia**. Easylinks at **donnaward.net**

Lesson 22~Symbols

Research and appropriately colour each symbol.

Prairie Crocus

Great Gray Owl

Symbols of the Shield
(give the meanings of the symbols on the shield)

Shield

Cross of St. George: _Manitoba's bond with Great britain_

Buffalo: _The importance of the Red River buffala and as a Prairie Province_

MANITOBA

While we may think of Manitoba as a prairie, farming province, only twelve percent of the land surface is agricultural land. There are three regions, the *Interior Plains*, the *Canadian Shield*, and the *Hudson Bay Lowland*.

Similar to Saskatchewan, the Natural Regions of the *Plains* includes three areas, however, there is far less Prairie land than in the neighbouring Prairie provinces. The *Prairie* has black soil which is best for grain crops. Almost completely grassland, the few natural trees cluster in creek gullies or stand like lonely sentinels in broad fields. Farmers plant rows of trees as windbreaks around houses and along the edges of farm fields. The *Prairie* is the driest region in Manitoba.

As you head north, the transitional *Aspen Parkland* blends natural forest with grassland and here as well, many field crops are grown.

The *Boreal Plains* reaches east as far as Lake Winnipeg and north just past the town of Flin Flon.

The largest geological region in Manitoba, the *Canadian Shield*, stretches from the bottom eastern corner of the province all the way to the top western corner.

> The northern towns of Thompson and Flin Flon were both founded after the discovery of minerals in these areas of the Shield. Flin Flon has the Saskatchewan/Manitoba border running right through the town.

The central area is the *Boreal Shield*. In the north, the forests give way to bare ground as trees become stunted and sparse in the *Taiga Shield*.

Around the shore of Hudson Bay, the *Hudson Bay Lowland* is a mixture of tidal flats, mossy swamp called muskeg, and flat, lichen covered ground. It is a cold, damp, treeless area.

Manitoba, like other prairie provinces, experiences extremes in weather. Since there are no mountains to block the air flow and no seas to moderate the temperature, summer

> Winnipeg, dubbed by some as Winterpeg, is famed for having the windiest corner in Canada, at the downtown intersection of Portage Avenue and Main Street.

> Churchill, popular as a place to view polar bears, is the only town in the Hudson Bay Lowland.

days can be extremely hot, especially on the Prairies. Winters can be severely cold, intensified by strong winds.

The clay soil of Manitoba does not immediately soak up rain water, causing it to sit in swampy pockets. What a great place for mosquitoes to breed! Manitobans laugh about the mosquitoes which they say are so big they can pick you up and carry you away. Maybe you have had an experience like the poet describes below.

A Mosquito in the Cabin

Although you bash her,
    swat her, smash her,
and go to bed victorious,
    happy and glorious
    she will come winging,
    zooming and zinging,
    wickedly singing
    over your bed.
You slap the air
    but she's in your hair
    cackling with laughter.
You smack your head,
    but she isn't dead -
    she's on the rafter.
She's out for blood -
    yours, my friend,
and she will get it, in the end.
She brings it first to boiling point,
    then lets it steam.
With a fee, fi, fo and contented fum
    she sips it
    while you dream.
Copyright Myra Stilborn. Used with permission.

Lesson 23~Geography

Write the appropriate numbers on the map below to show the location of these geological regions.

Plains	**1**
Canadian Shield	**2**
Hudson Bay Lowland	**3**

Colour the two small maps.

Using an atlas, mark the following places on the map below.

Winnipeg	Lake Winnipeg
Brandon	Red River
Flin Flon	Assiniboine River
Thompson	Nelson River
Churchill	Churchill River

Geological Regions

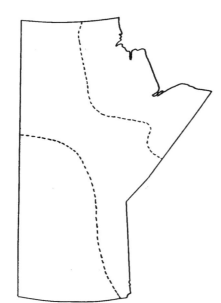

Natural Regions

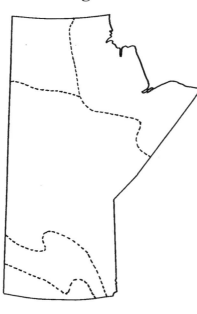

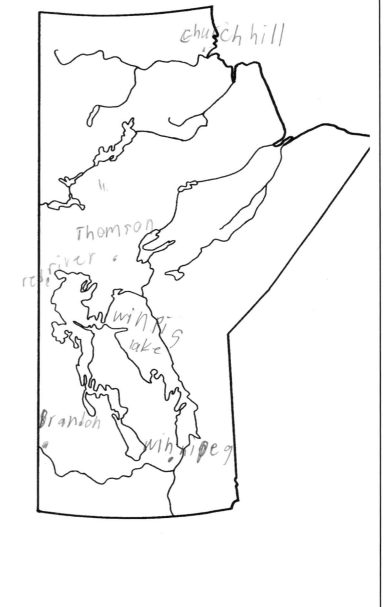

Canada . . . is . . . a garden into which have been transplanted the hardiest and brightest of flowers from many lands, each retaining in its new environment the best of the qualities for which it was loved and prized in its native land.[1]

Honourable John G. Diefenbaker, when Prime Minister of Canada

Canada is a nation of immigrants. Even the First Nations descended from travellers who migrated across the Bering Strait. During the time of European exploration, French newcomers dominated colonies in the northern New World. Later, American Loyalists, Scottish settlers, and Irish famine victims swelled the ranks of the English speaking population. While some immigrants arrived from eastern countries like Japan, China, and India, entry was restricted because of racial prejudice.

In 1966, Canadian government policy (defined in the White Paper) put an end to government discrimination based on colour, race, or religion. It stated that immigrants would be accepted if: 1) they had family members already in Canada; 2) they had skills for jobs available in Canada; or 3) they were refugees from war or danger. Thus, racial bias was not an allowable factor in the granting of Canadian citizenship.

The Official Languages Act, passed in 1969, stated that both French and English were authorized languages, making Canada a *bilingual* country. In 1971 the government announced its policy to recognize ethnic groups and officially declare Canada a *multicultural* country. Prime Minister Pierre Trudeau stated:

The government will support and encourage the various cultures and ethnic groups that give structure and vitality to our society. They will be encouraged to share their cultural expression and values with other Canadians and so contribute to a richer life for us all. [2]

So what did this mean to Canadians? Immigrants were, and still are, encouraged to retain their cultural heritage, customs, and mother-tongue. Consequently, many Canadians describe their identity in terms such as Chinese-Canadian, French-Canadian, or African-Canadian.

Mother-tongue: This term refers to a person's own language which is learned in childhood. ESL- Acronym for "English as a Second Language." ESL classes for immigrants are funded by the provinces.

1 John W. Friesen, *When Cultures Clash, Case Studies in Multiculturalism* (Calgary: Detselig Enterprises Ltd., 1985), p. 2.

2 *Ibid., p. 3*

The government gives financial grants to help groups celebrate and retain their language and heritage in order to prevent its loss with future generations. Cultural neighbourhoods, programs, and festivals keep alive racial distinctions.

There is a richness to understanding cultures from around the world. Preserving one's roots brings a positive self-identity to people. On the other hand, some immigrants feel isolated within their cultural group, when their desire was to become completely Canadian.

Most Canadians enjoy learning the customs of other cultures and accept ethnic Canadians without discrimination. Revinder Tulsiani, an immigrant from India says this:

> When I first enrolled in school I didn't make a lot of friends, because I couldn't speak the language. The big kids would steal my lunch and I was afraid to tell anyone because I was small and skinny. I was called names like "Paki" and "Ravioli" because I was different . . . . However, over the years that I've been here I have seen discrimination almost disappear from my life and those around me.
>
> Now I think that Canada is a perfect example of what Gandhi taught Indians throughout his life, that people of different cultures could live together in harmony. While maintaining their own heritage, they could learn to gain from other cultures around them.
>
> Isn't that what Canadian sociologists call the "salad bowl theory"? The Canadian way of life. . . gives all its members the opportunity to preserve their heritage while taking in the new identity of a Canadian; a tolerant, hard-working, contributing member of a free society which cares. [1]

Multi-cultural celebrations are popular around the province of Manitoba. The biggest is the summer event called Folkorama, where people can experience food and dance from around the world. The *Festival du Voyageur* is Canada's 2nd largest winter carnival next to the one in Quebec City. Winnipeg is said to have the largest French-speaking community outside the province of Quebec.

Who snowshoed 2,800 kilometers?

In the winter of 1816, Jean Baptist Lagimodiere walked and snowshoed 2,800 kilometers from Winnipeg to Montreal. He brought the news to Lord Selkirk that his Red River Colony had been attacked.

---

[1] Robert Livesey, *Coming to Canada* (Oakville: Little Brick Schoolhouse Inc., 1994), pp. 120-122.

Lesson 24~Multiculturalism

1.   For what reason were people from Japan and China restricted from immigrating in Canada's early years?

Because of racial prejudice

2.   Immigrants must qualify in one of three categories. What are the three categories that allow them to be accepted into Canada with immigrant status?

They had family members already in canada.
They had skills for jobs avaliable in canada
They were refugees from war or danger

3.   What changed in Canada with the Official Languages Act of 1969?

that both french and English were
authorized langes

4.   Name two things immigrants are encouraged to retain through multiculturalism?

their culture expressions and values with
other canadians and so contribute to a richer
life for us all

5.   Name both good results and negative results of multiculturalism.

That people of different cultures could live together:

Population

Manitoba: 1,119,583
Winnipeg: 706,900 (provincial capital)

The Red River Floods

A (USA) farmer . . . slogged through waist-deep water, carrying his ten-year-old daughter to higher ground. "I hope you Canadians are ready," he said. "You have no idea what's coming." [1]

Winding its way north towards Hudson Bay, the Red River has been known for spring floods, but when it destroyed the town of Grand Forks, North Dakota, in April, 1997, the people of Manitoba knew this was no ordinary spring overflow. In horror they watched news casts as the flood made its way across the Canadian border. Volunteers joined the Armed Forces in packing sand bags to make dikes around towns and homes.

Some towns survived, like Emerson at the Canada/US border, where the water outside the dike was higher than the 2nd story windows of houses inside. But other homesteads and towns were not so lucky. Though the 500 people of Ste. Agathe thought they were safe, they evacuated the town as a precaution. That night water rushed through a hole in the dike and by morning, the water in the streets was two meters deep. When the water reached the city of Winnipeg, the protection of floodways and a hastily built dike held fast. While there were many losses, there were also many victories over "the flood of the century."

Internet Links: **CBC Archives**/Disasters and Tragedies/ Extreme Weather. Segment 8 & 11 shows the Hamblin family preparing for the flood. Easylinks at **donnaward.**

History Highlights

	Plains and Subarctic Natives dwell in the land
1670	Hudson's Bay Company formed
1682	York Factory becomes first fur-trading post in Manitoba
1812	Lord Selkirk brings settlers to the Red River
1870	Manitoba joins Confederation
1896-1914	Many immigrants arrive to settle in Manitoba

The Nonsuch - first ship to trade in Hud-

Red-river Cart used by Selkirk settlers.

Winnipeg, Hub of the Wheel

Manitoba is the only province dominated by one central city. Winnipeg houses over 60% of the province's total population.

Winnie-the-Pooh

A World War I Army officer from Winnipeg, travelling through Ontario, bought an orphaned bear cub and named her Winnie, after Winnipeg. The cub, a favourite mascot, went to England with the regiment. Later, as a popular attraction of the London Zoo, she became an inspiration for the fictitious bear character, Winnie-the-Pooh.

[1] Jake MacDonald and Shirley Sandre, *Faces of the Flood.* (Toronto: 1997), p. 17.

Colour the population bar graph.
See library books on Manitoba (adult & children's library section 917.12).
Also: Jake MacDonald and Shirley Sandre, *Faces of the Flood.* (1997).
Winnipeg Free Press, *A Red Sea Rising* (1997).

ONTARIO
LAND OF
SPARKLING WATERS

Land of the silver birch
Home of the beaver
Where still the mighty moose
Wanders at will
Blue lake and rocky shore
I will return once more
Boom didi-a-da, boom didi-a-da,
Boom didi-a-da, boom.

There on a rocky ledge
I'll build my wigwam
Close to the water's edge
Silent and still
Blue lake and rocky shore
I will return once more
Boom didi-a-da, boom didi-a-da
Boom didi-a-da, boom

Anonymous
Ontario campfire song

The Iroquoian word "kanadario" means "shining lake" or "sparkling waters." Since almost 20% of the area is beautiful lakes and rivers, the adaptation of *Ontario* from that aboriginal word is a fitting name for this province.

Common Loon

The melancholy laugh of the Common Loon is the sound campers love. Coming in pairs from their southern migrating grounds, loons settle on solitary lakes in the Canadian north to rear their brood. They take turns incubating the two eggs. A few hours after birth the young nestle on their parents' backs for outings on the lake. Loons are excellent divers and swimmers, hunting fish until the lakes freeze and they have to head south once again.

The tenderfoot on his first venture into lake country soon hears loons, and for the rest of his life will never forget them. Nothing else is like them. Their sounds are wild and shrill and eerie with a touch of madness, heard often enough to be known to every northern traveller, ... To lie awake with the music of loons can be to glimpse in essence the lure of the north woods. Both loon and land are free and untamed, alive, unique and harsh. Anyone who has canoed the north or walked its trails will go suddenly thoughtful at the sound of loons. [1]

Internet Links: Listen to the song of the Loon at **Cornell Lab of Ornithology**. Watch a video of the loon at **Hinterland Who's Who**. Easylinks at **donnaward.net**

---

[1] R. Yorke Edwards "The Proof of Wildness: Where Caribou Still Stand," Bordon Spears (ed.), *Wilderness Canada (Toronto: Clarke, Irwin & Company Ltd., 1970), p. 154.*

White Trillium

In April and May the White Trillium blooms in the shaded woodlands of the mixed forest, its three petals delicate against the forest greenery.

Economy

Ontario is the country's leading manufacturing province, producing 50% of Canada's total goods. Automobile production is the most important industry, next to the building of machinery. Canada's financial institutions, banks, insurance companies and other corporations, have head offices in Toronto, making it the financial centre of Canada.

Why is the McIntosh apple Canadian?

The most important fruit crop in Canada is the apple, and the most renowned is the McIntosh. Apples were first brought to Canada from France in 1606. In 1811, an Ontario settler named John McIntosh discovered a wild apple tree at an abandoned farm near his home. He transplanted it onto his farm. The fruit was the best he had ever eaten. Since apple seeds don't produce the exact same variety of tree, McIntosh had to learn the art of grafting. Soon his son was selling branches of the tree all around the area. The original tree stopped bearing fruit in 1906. Now today, every McIntosh apple tree and every McIntosh apple are descendents of that first tree on John McIntosh's farm.

Lesson 26~Symbols

Research and appropriately colour each symbol.

White Trillium

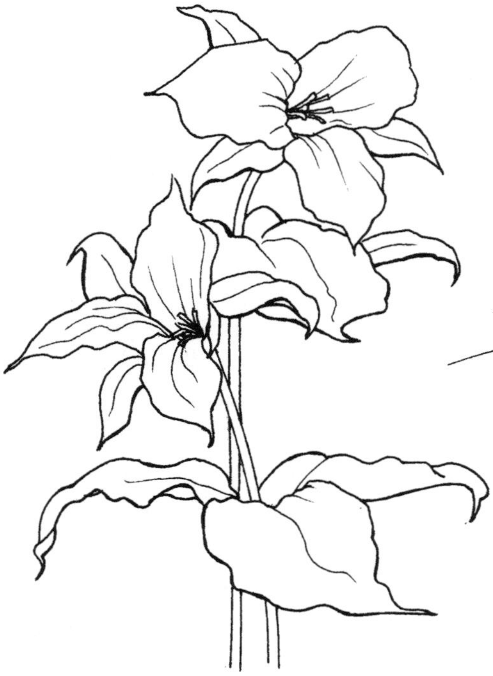

Common Loon

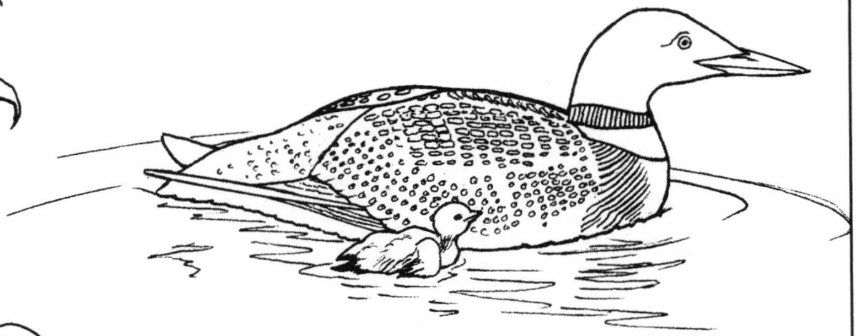

Symbols of the Shield

(give the meanings of the symbols on the shield)

Cross of St. George: ____________________

____

Maple Leaves: ____________________

____

Shield

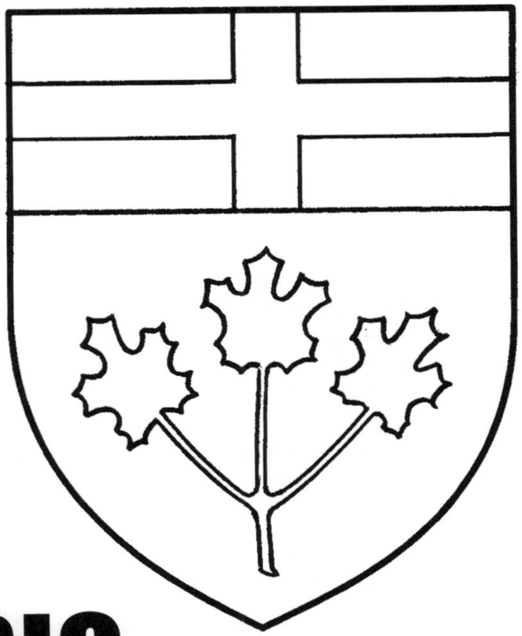

ONTARIO

Two terms are loaded with meaning to those who live in Ontario, bringing clear visions to mind of the two main geographical regions. "Northern Ontario" speaks of lakes, rock, pine, wilderness, and for some, the fond memories of "cottage country." The *Canadian Shield* and the *Hudson Bay Lowland* dominate the north. "Southern Ontario" is the warmer area of mixed wood forests, large cities, industry, and farmland. This is the geological region of the *Great Lakes Lowland.*

The *Great Lakes Lowland* of Southern Ontario holds Ontario's best farmland and the majority of the population. The land is fairly level and has a long growing season. Once a land of mixed-wood forest, towns, cities and farms now dominate the landscape.   The *Canadian Shield* to the north, covers two-thirds of the province and is a mixture of Boreal Forest, bare rock, lakes, and swamps. The land is so rugged that it was almost as difficult to build the railway through the Canadian Shield as it was through the western mountains. Granite had to be blasted and levelled, which, in many areas, revealed a wealth of minerals for future miners.

The *Hudson Bay Lowland*, just south of Hudson Bay and James Bay, is a swampy quagmire of muskeg like that in Manitoba. This bleak, water-soaked region offers a prime breeding ground for nasty biting flies and mosquitoes, but is also a haven for many types of waterfowl.

Weather patterns blow into Ontario from the west. The extremes in temperature are often moderated in the south by the Great Lakes as water cools and warms more slowly than air. This moderating effect can keep southern Ontario cooler in summer and warmer in winter than the prairie provinces. Certain areas of Ontario, called snowbelts, receive far more precipitation than other areas, especially in winter, because of their location and relationship to the Great Lakes. Northern temperatures are dramatically cooler than in the south.

Is Lake Superior the largest lake in Canada?

Lake Superior, at 82,107 square kilometers, is the largest freshwater lake in the world. However, only part of the lake is in Canada. The rest is in the United States. The biggest lake completely surrounded by Canadian land is Great Bear Lake in the Northwest Territories which has 31,328 square kilometers of water surface. The second largest lake completely in Canada is Great Slave Lake, at 28,570 square kilometers.

Internet Links: Ontario quizzes at **Fun Trivia.** Relief map at **Canada Info Link**. Easylinks at **donnaward.net**

Has Niagara Falls ever dried up?

The only time both the American Falls and Horseshoe Falls stopped flowing was on March 29, 1848, when an ice jam on Lake Erie, near Buffalo, blocked the water that flowed into the Niagara River. People dared to walk across the rocks above and below the falls. At the bottom of the falls, people picked up bayonets, swords, tomahawks and other mementos from the War of 1812. On March 31, the ice broke up and water roared like a wall down the riverbed and over the falls. Since 1964, steps have been taken to prevent ice blockages which would cause damage to hydroelectric equipment below the falls.

Lesson 2~Geography

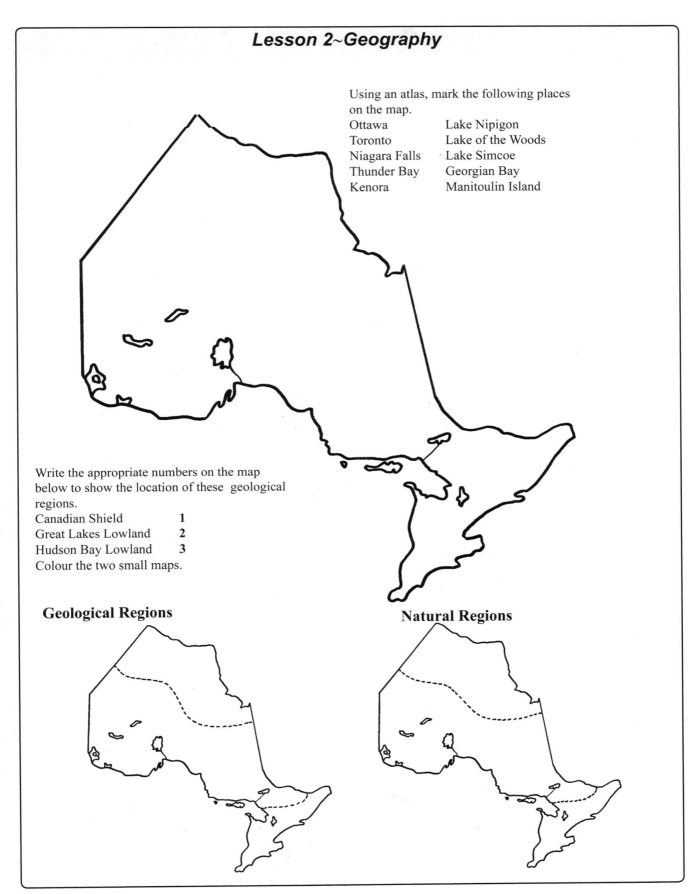

Using an atlas, mark the following places on the map.

Ottawa   Lake Nipigon
Toronto   Lake of the Woods
Niagara Falls   Lake Simcoe
Thunder Bay   Georgian Bay
Kenora   Manitoulin Island

Write the appropriate numbers on the map below to show the location of these geological regions.

Canadian Shield   **1**
Great Lakes Lowland   **2**
Hudson Bay Lowland   **3**
Colour the two small maps.

Geological Regions

Natural Regions

A large percentage of Canadian manufacturing takes place in Ontario and Quebec, especially along the St. Lawrence Seaway and the Great Lakes. The area around the southwest end of Lake Ontario, where Toronto and Hamilton are located, is nicknamed "The Golden Horseshoe" because of all the industries and businesses situated there.

What do manufacturers look for when choosing a site for their industry? They want to make the most profit with the least expense, therefore, they choose a site close to: 1) raw materials; 2) inexpensive transportation and; 3) large cities where they sell their goods. The St. Lawrence and Great Lakes Seaway is an easy route for transporting raw materials and finished goods. The large population in Ontario, Quebec, and the eastern United States provide a good market at short distances.

One of the most important *primary* industries in Ontario, steel making, brings millions of dollars into the province. The necessary raw materials such as iron ore, coal, and limestone are within easy access by rail and water. The biggest steel companies, at Hamilton and Sault Ste. Marie, are located close to water transportation. Automobile production is Ontario's major *secondary* industry. Large auto assembly plants employ many people, but of the 900 companies in Canada, most make only parts for the cars and trucks.

How many ships use the Welland Canal?

The St. Lawrence River and the Great Lakes shipping route once had an impassable barrier between Lake Ontario and Lake Erie - Niagara Falls! The Welland Canal was built in 1829 to bypass the falls. Today, more than 4,000 ships pass through the locks in a season. The canal is 42 km long, has 7 lift locks and covers a height difference of almost 100 metres.

How does the percentage of manufacturing of each province relate to percentage of population?

PROVINCE/TERRITORY	VALUE OF MANUFACTURING Percentage	POPULATION Percentage
Ontario	52.6	36.4
Quebec	24.0	25.4
British Columbia	8.8	12.0
Alberta	7.1	9.4
New Brunswick	2.1	2.8
Manitoba	2.0	4.0
Nova Scotia	1.5	3.4
Saskatchewan	1.3	3.6
Newfoundland	0.3	2.1
Prince Edward Island	0.2	0.5
The Territories	0.1	0.4
	Total: 100%	100%

Statistics Canada, Cat. No. 11-001E, 1995

Lesson 28~Manufacturing

1.   Manufacturers want to make the most profit with the least expenses. What are the three things they consider when choosing an industry site?

raw materials

inexpensive transportation

large cities where they cell thier good.

2.   What transportation route do manufacturers from Ontario and Quebec use to get their goods to market? What method of transportation are they using and why?

The st larwance and Great Lakes seaway.

4.   What is Ontario's most important primary industry and where are the largest of these industries located?

steel making

Hamilton and sault ste marie.

5.   Use the information from the chart in your text to make a line graph. Plot the numbers on the graph for the percentage of manufacturing in each province, and join the points with one colour. Do the same for percentage of population and join the points with another colour.

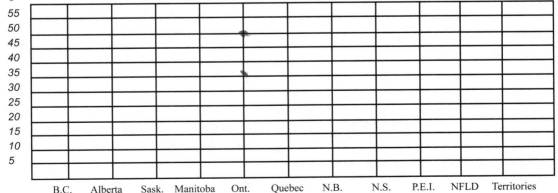

Population

Ontario: 11,410,046
Toronto: 5,304,100 (provincial capital)

The Dionne Quintuplets

An outstanding event happened during the night of May 28, 1934, that changed the small northern town of Corbeil, Ontario, forever. Five tiny, frail, but identical baby girls came into the world in the farmhouse of a French-Canadian couple, Oliva and Elzire Dionne.

Since the babies were the world's first surviving quintuplets, there was great public interest in them.

Convinced that only a doctor could handle such a unique case, the Ontario government built a special nursery, putting Dr. Dafoe in charge of the girls rather than their own parents. A public observation garden accompanied the nursery and, over time, more than 3 million visitors came to gaze at them.

After 9 years of legal battles, their father was finally able to get them home, but a rift had developed. They didn't adjust to the family. As adults, the sisters moved together to Montreal.

In the spring of 1998, the 3 surviving quints were awarded an apology and financial compensation for the way the government mistreated them in their childhood.

History Highlights

	Various aboriginal groups dwell in land
1648	Jesuits build Ste-Marie Among the Hurons Mission
1763	Hurons and mission destroyed by Iroquois
1791	New France defeated by British Quebec; divided into Upper (Ontario) & Lower Canada (Quebec)
1812	War of 1812
1837	William L. Mackenzie's unsuccessful rebellion
1841	Upper & Lower Canada becomes United Province of Canada
1854	Railroads built
1867	At Confederation, Ontario is one of first four provinces in the Dominion of Canada

Niagara Escarpment

The Niagara Escarpment is a long ridge of rock that crosses southern Ontario from the tip of the Bruce Peninsula on Lake Huron to Niagara Falls. The Niagara River, cutting through the escarpment, is what forms Niagara Falls. At the north end, the Bruce Trail contains some of the most beautiful hiking trails and ski areas in the province.

Was the first long distance telephone call made in Canada?

The first long distance telephonic communication was made in Ontario between Brantford and Paris, a distance of 12 kilometers.

Colour the population bar graph.
See library books on Ontario (adult & children's library section 917.13).

QUEBEC
PLACE WHERE THE
RIVER
NARROWS

"My first day in Canada remains vividly etched in my memory. It was October. Yousuf had taken me hiking in the Gatineau Hills, where the trees seemed on fire with brilliant autumn foliage. I had never imagined that such glorious colours were possible. That first impression had a profound influence in shaping my future life."

Malek. *Canada, The Land That Shapes Us.*
(Toronto: Key Porter Books Ltd., 1995).

U N I T   N I N E

Look at the St. Lawrence River on a map of Canada. Notice at the site of Quebec City how the river narrows dramatically. The people of the First Nations called it "Kebec," meaning "place where the river narrows." That is the name Samuel de Champlain chose when he built the first French settlement there in 1608. In the end, the whole province became known as Quebec.

Snowy Owl

The Snowy Owl, almost pure white, lives in the far north on the Tundra. At nesting time, it lines a shallow depression in the tundra with moss and lays its egg there on the ground. Its thick coat of feathers even covers its legs to help it survive in the Arctic. The Snowy Owl does not migrate south.

There was a young man of Quebec
Who was frozen in snow to his neck,
When asked, "Are you friz?"
He replied, "Yes, I is,
But we don't call this cold in Quebec."

Anonymous
(once attributed to Rudyard Kipling)

Madonna Lily

One of the most fragrant of the garden lilies, the white Madonna Lily, was chosen as Quebec's provincial flower because of its similarity to the fleur-de-lis on the Quebec flag. Although it originally came from Europe, this white lily can be easily grown in the warmer zones in Canada.

Economy

Montreal, one of the biggest manufacturing centres in Canada, produces clothing, food, pulp and paper, and many other goods. Quebec's only farmland, the St. Lawrence Lowland, is suitable for Canada's largest dairy industry. Almost 40% of Quebec's agriculture is dairy while the rest is fruits and vegetables, and mixed farms. Feed crops are grown for the farm animals.

Who was the strongest man ever?

Louis Noe Cyr of Napierville, Quebec, was the strongest man able to lift 1967 kg.

What is La Francophonie?

La Francophonie is the alliance of the French-speaking countries. Of the 38 countries represented, most are former colonies of France. Quebec is a member of La Francophonie.

Internet Links: Listen to the sound of the Snowy Owl at **Cornell Lab of Ornithology**. Easylinks at **donnaward. net**

Lesson 30~Symbols

Research and appropriately colour each symbol.

White Garden Lily

Snowy Owl

Symbols of the Shield
(give the meanings of the symbols on the shield)

Fleur-de-lis: French kings

Gold Lion: great britain.

Maple Leaves: canada

Shield

QUEBEC

Quebec is by far the largest province in Canada. The majority of the population lives along the St. Lawrence River in the *St. Lawrence Lowland*. Most of Quebec lies in the inhospitable *Canadian Shield* region.

The *Canadian Shield* area covers nearly 90% of the whole province. Still wilderness, it contains almost a million lakes and some of Canada's mightiest flowing rivers. The vegetation of the Shield is bare Tundra in the north, with only lichens and some dwarf birch or willow. The marshes on the Tundra provide a sanctuary for many birds who feed on the swarms of insects in spring and summer. Barren-ground caribou travel the Tundra in large herds.

South of the Tundra, the transitional Taiga Shield is a mixture of bare rock and evergreen trees. Further south, in the Boreal Shield, the trees survive better and provide hectares of softwood suitable for Quebec's pulp and paper industry. A variety of minerals is harvested from the rock in this area of the Canadian Shield.

The *St. Lawrence Lowland* contains the province's best farmland. Level terrain, fertile earth, and lots of precipitation make this a rich agricultural area. The maples of the Mixed Wood Forest provide brilliant fall colours and spring sap for maple syrup.

Rising oddly in the flat landscape, the remains of eight ancient volcanoes, called the Monteregian hills, can be seen in the southwest part of the Lowland. Mount Royal, around which Montreal is situated, is the most well-known. On either side of the mouth of the St. Lawrence River, the Appalachian Mountains are visible in the rough terrain on the Gaspe Peninsula and as they stretch northeast toward Newfoundland. North of the river they are called the Laurentian Mountains, or Laurentides.

Southern Quebec is an area in which cold, arctic winds meet warmer air from the south creating a tremendous amount of precipitation. Snow dumped on the Laurentides makes it a great winter playground for skiers, but the snow also means city dwellers have to shovel continually. Over an average winter, there may be as much as two or more metres of snowfall. (Measure that! That is a lot of snow!) In the north, there is less precipitation and colder temperatures.

Internet Links: Quebec geography quiz at **Fun Trivia**. Relief map at **Canada Info Link**. Go to **donnaward.net**

The Canadian Passion - Hockey

While lacrosse is the national summer sport, hockey is Canada's national winter sport. The game, invented by Canadians, is now played in at least twenty other countries. The NHL (National Hockey League) was formed in 1917 with three Canadian teams. By the 1940s, Toronto and Montreal were the only Canadian cities with teams and the rest were in the USA Most of the players however, were Canadian. Today, Canada produces 60 percent of the players in the NHL.

Country of Origin of NHL players		
Country	Players	Percentage
Canada	405	60.3
United States	99	14.3
Russia	46	6.9
Czech Rep.	38	5.7
Sweden	16	5.0
Finland	11	1.6
Slovakia	11	1.6
Latvia	4	0.6
Ukraine	4	0.3
England	2	0.3
Germany	2	0.3
Lithuania	2	0.3
Poland	2	0.3
Belarus	1	0.1
Nigeria	1	0.1
N. Ireland	1	0.1
Scotland	1	0.1
South Africa	1	0.1
South Korea	1	0.1
Total	671	99.7

NHL players per province/territory	
Province	Players
Ontario	164
Quebec	76
Alberta	60
British Columbia	42
Saskatchewan	34
Manitoba	18
Nova Scotia	4
New Brunswick	3
Newfoundland	3
Northwest Terr.	1
P.E.I.	0
Yukon	0

Figures taken from *Canadian Geographic*, March/April 1999

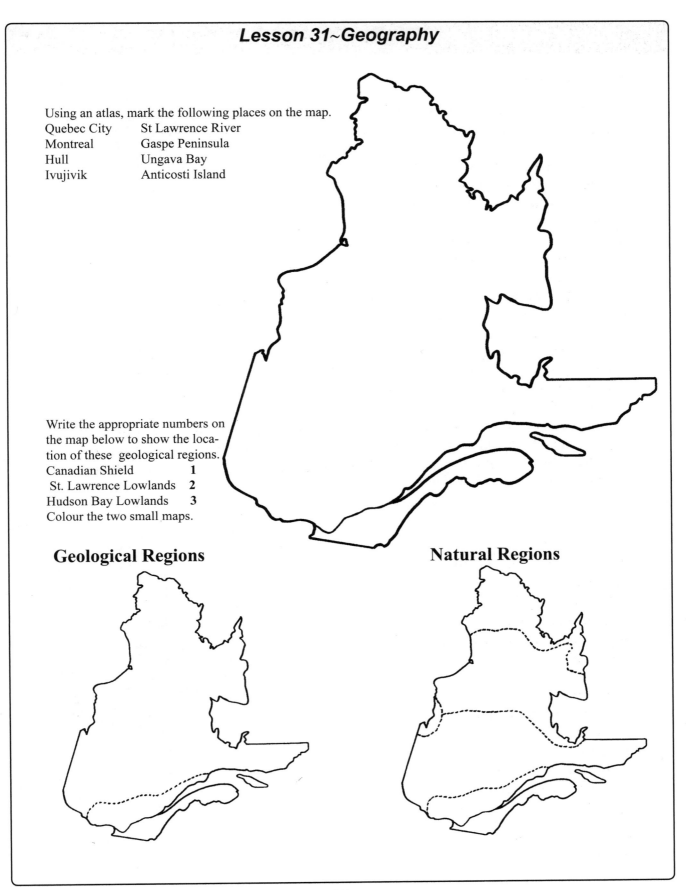

Using an atlas, mark the following places on the map.

Quebec City   St Lawrence River
Montreal   Gaspe Peninsula
Hull   Ungava Bay
Ivujivik   Anticosti Island

Write the appropriate numbers on the map below to show the location of these geological regions.

Canadian Shield   **1**
 St. Lawrence Lowlands   **2**
Hudson Bay Lowlands   **3**
Colour the two small maps.

Geological Regions

Natural Regions

Hydroelectric Power

In the early years, the settlers harnessed the energy in moving water with water-wheels, which powered grist mills for grinding grain into flour and saw mills for cutting logs. The invention of the *generator*, which can change mechanical energy into electricity, combined with a waterwheel, or *turbine*, made it possible to use falling water to produce electricity. This is known as *hydroelectricity*.

Canada's abundance of rivers gives us the ability to produce relatively inexpensive hydroelectricity. This is our main *renewable* source of energy. If you look at the incredible number of rivers in Canada, you can see why our country is a world leader in the production of hydroelectric power.

Many of the rivers start in highland areas or mountains. A large amount of precipitation and steep drops in elevation provide ideal locations for hydroelectric plants.

Quebec generates more hydroelectric power than any other province - almost half of Canada's hydroelectricity. Hydro-Quebec built a number of extensive projects in northern Quebec which supply the large population in southern Quebec as well as markets in the United States.

In 1971, Hydro-Quebec began the controversial James Bay Project, a series of dams which diverts some rivers to fill up others. Forests were flooded as new lakes were formed. Some streams became huge rivers, while others dried up. Power plants built along the rivers create vast amounts of hydroelectricity for the southern population. Plans for future development are challenged by environmentalists and the First Nations (Cree) because of the massive changes it makes to the environment.

Since most of the power plants close to the cities have become inadequate, there will continually be a push towards northern waters for hydro electrical power.

Ice Storm

The first morning the shimmering, ice-covered trees created a fairytale scene, but after 5 days of freezing rain, Quebec and Ontario looked like a war zone. Huge hydro towers sat crumpled on the ground; trees and telephone poles were toppled, littering the land with branches, wires, crushed cars and debris. When the ice storm began in January, 1998, no one guessed it would be the most destructive weather disaster recorded in Canada.

Over 5 million people experienced a lack of hydro power resulting in a loss of heat,

lights, and crucial farm equipment such as milking machines. In some neighbourhoods, it took 33 days to restore power. Quebec residents were hit the hardest.

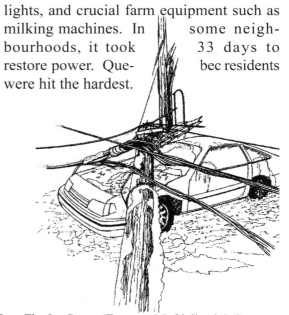

See, *The Ice Storm* (Toronto: McClelland & Steward Inc., 1998).

Internet Links: See news footage of the ice storm at **CBC Archives**/Disasters and Tragedies/Extreme Weather. Easylinks at **donnaward.net**

Lesson 32~Hydroelectric Power

1. How did early settlers use water to make power? What did they use the energy for?

    water wheels   to grind wheat and   cut logs

    _____

2. What invention made it possible to harness water to make hydroelectricity?

    generator

3. What natural feature in Canada allows the country to produce hydroelectricity?

    rivers

4. Which province produces the most hydroelectricity and what is the name of the large hydroelectric project in that province?

    quebec   james bay

    _____

5. Why will there be a continual push for power plant sites in the north?

    most of the power plants close to the cities
    have become inadequate.

Population

Quebec: 7,237,479
Quebec City: 717,600 (provincial capital)
Montreal: 3,720,000

Quebec: A Distinct Society

At the time of Confederation, English and Scottish men owned most of the businesses while French Canadians were the underpaid workers. French Canadians increasingly felt dissatisfied. The unrest was evident in the Rebellion of 1867 which was put down by British soldiers. In the 1960s, in a time called the Quiet Revolution, the provincial government made many dramatic changes in the way Quebec was ruled, giving French Canadians a new role in Canada. The idea of separation from the rest of Canada began to take root. French Canadians in Quebec began to call themselves *Quebecois*.

The Quebec provincial government continually wrestled with the federal government in Ottawa over political power. In 1970, a terrorist group called the *Front de Liberation du Quebec (FLQ)* set off several bombs in Montreal, and kidnapped two politicians. One of the men, Pierre Laporte, was killed by the FLQ.

In 1974, French was made the official language of Quebec, and in 1977 a law was passed to make it the everyday language of work and education. This move meant that immigrants to Quebec had to go to French schools rather than learn English as their second language. All public signs including business and road signs had to be in French.

Rene Levesque, the leader of the separatist group called the *Parti Quebecois*, was

History Highlights

1608	Champlain builds a post at Quebec City
1759	British troops conquer New France by taking Quebec City
1763	New France becomes a British Colony, called Quebec
1791	Quebec Act guarantees use of the French language and Catholic religion
1841	Upper and Lower Canada are named
1867	At Confederation Quebec becomes one of the four first provinces in the Dominion of Canada

voted into the provincial government in 1976 and the quest for independence began in earnest. The Parti Quebecois hoped most Quebecers wanted separation. In 1980, a special vote called a referendum, showed that 60% of the people of Quebec chose to stay with Canada. Another referendum on separation was defeated in 1995.

The future is still uncertain, but for some time yet, Quebec will remain an integral part of the country of Canada.

> We are French Canadians, but our country is not confined to the territory overshadowed by the citadel of Quebec; our country is Canada, it is the whole of what is covered by the British flag on the American continent, the fertile lands bordered by the Bay of Fundy, the Valley of the St. Lawrence, the region of the Great Lakes, the prairies of the West, the Rocky Mountains, the lands washed by the famous ocean where breezes are said to be as sweet as the breezes of the Mediterranean.
>
> Wilfrid Laurier, future Prime Minister, address in Quebec City, June 24, 1889. Ulric Barthe (ed), *Wilfrid Laurier on the Platform: 1871-1890 (1890)*

Colour the population bar graph.
See library books on Quebec (adult & children's library section 917.14).
Also: Gazette, The (Montreal). *The Ice Storm.* (1998).

NEW BRUNSWICK THE PICTURE PROVINCE

We saw everything we'd come to see: glimpses of far, shimmering lakes, and strong rivers that tumbled away toward east and west; and ridge upon ridge of bristling, green forests, stretching for county after county until they vanished into a hazy skyline. New Brunswick boasts about its mysterious panthers, big tides, big forests, big sand bars, big salmon, and if they're colourful, even its politicians. I've known for nearly four decades: when you're travelling in New Brunswick, just about anything is possible.

Dudley Witney and Harry Bruce. *Atlantic Canada.*
(Toronto: Key Porter Books, 1991).

The rolling hills of the Appalachians, rushing rivers and scenic coastlines, have contributed to New Brunswick's nickname, the Picture Province. Named for the royal family of Brunswick, it was one of the four original provinces to make up the Dominion of Canada.

Black-capped Chickadee

The Black-capped Chickadee, a year-round resident of woodlands across Canada is one of the smallest birds able to survive the harsh winters. Small flocks rove the frozen woodlands, hopping all day from branch to branch, looking for dormant insects, spider eggs and cocoons, and seeds and berries.

In spring their cheery song can be heard as flocks break up and pair off to mate and raise young. Rearing one or two broods together each season, chickadees sometimes mate for life. Their cheery *chick-a-dee-dee-dee* song brightens the woodlands as they look for food.

Naturalist, R.D. Lawrence, recalls the chickadees which readily took seeds from his hand.
"If I have such a thing as a favourite bird, it must be the chickadee! I have met them all over the continent and they always gladden the heart. They are, in my view, the most trusting of all the birds, and they are among the most agile and enduring, braving the northland winters when few others their size can survive." [1]

Internet Links: Listen to the Black Capped Chickadee at **Cornell Lab of Ornithology**. Watch a video at **Hinterland Who's Who**. Easylinks at **donnaward.net**

Purple Violet

The delicate blossoms of the Purple Violet are a delight to those who love spring flowers. They brighten gardens, marshy lands and cool woodlots with their tiny, pansy like blooms.

Economy

Ninety percent of New Brunswick is still covered by forest; so, it is easy to see why this is the province's most valuable resource. About 25% of all goods made in New Brunswick are related to the forest industry. Mining, fishing and farming also add to the health of the economy.

"As Canadian as . . ."

How would you complete that phrase?
Peter C. Newman, noted author, editor and journalist, ran a contest when he was the editor of Maclean's, asking Canadians to complete the phrase "As Canadian as . . ."
Some ideas were "As Canadian as the beaver," or "As Canadian as maple syrup." The winning phrase was: "As Canadian as possible under the circumstances." What does this tell you about Canadians?

---

[1] R.D. Lawrence. *Wildlife in North America: Bird.* (Don Mills: Thomas Nelson Ltd, 1974), p. 98.

Lesson 34~Symbols

Research and appropriately colour each symbol.

Purple Violet

Black-capped Chickadee

Symbols of the Shield

(give the meanings of the symbols on the shield)

Gold Lion:_____

_____

Ship:_____

_____

Shield

NEW BRUNSWICK

New Brunswick, part of the *Appalachian Mountain Region,* has two upland areas and a coastal plain. Much of the province contains rolling mountains. A large percentage of the land is untamed; covered in mixed forest called the Acadian Forest.

The highest area in New Brunswick, the *Central Highlands*, is rocky and heavily forested. A number of New Brunswick's many rivers have their source in these rugged hills. The Miramichi River and the Restigouche River are both known for the salmon that leap the waterfalls on their way to up river spawning grounds. The St. John River runs all the way from the northwest down to the cold Bay of Fundy in the south.

The other upland area, the *Southern Highlands*, overlooks the cliffs carved by the monstrous tides of the Bay of Fundy. At Hopewell Cape, large sandstone rocks, five stories high, rise from the ocean floor, carved by tides into strange shapes. At high tide, only the trees and the tops of the rocks are visible, so they are called the Flowerpot Islands. All along the Fundy Coast the Highlands contain beautiful scenery.

Although New Brunswick does not have very much farmland, the river valleys of the Coastal Lowlands offer rich soil, moist conditions and a temperate climate. Along the coast are peat bogs, spongy marshes and sand dunes.

The weather in the Central Highlands is largely affected by the continental climate to the west, so that temperatures are more extreme than in the coastal areas. The ocean keeps the coastal temperatures moderate. A lot of fog is produced in the Bay of Fundy, especially in spring and early summer as warm air from the land meets the cooler air over the bay.

The rock formations at Hopewell Cape are fascinating at low tide.

Internet Links: Find out why Fundy tides are the highest in the world. Go to **Hopewell Rocks.** See **Fun Trivia** for Atlantic Provinces Quizzes. Easylinks at **donnaward.net**

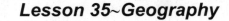

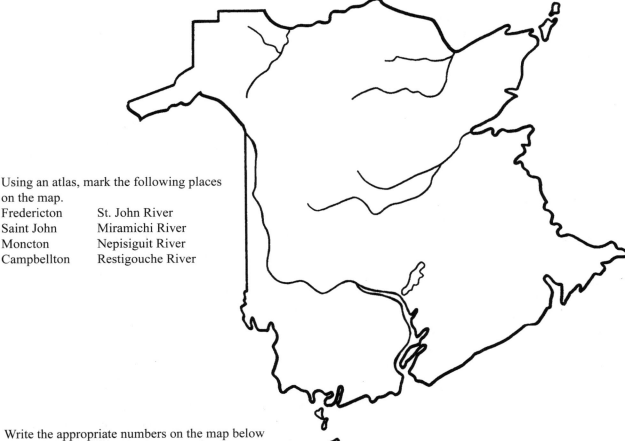

Using an atlas, mark the following places on the map.

Fredericton	St. John River
Saint John	Miramichi River
Moncton	Nepisiguit River
Campbellton	Restigouche River

Write the appropriate numbers on the map below to show the location of these geological regions.

Central Highlands	1
Southern Highlands	2
Coastal Lowlands	3

Colour the two small maps.

Geological Regions

Natural Regions

Secret and elusive, the cougar is a solitary hunter that is rarely seen by humans. The largest wild cat in Canada, the cougar prefers deer for food, but will also prey on small mammals. At one time, cougars ranged across our entire continent, but by 1900, they were considered *extirpated* in eastern North America. Hunters prized their fur and farmers killed them to protect livestock. The cougar still inhabits remote areas in the western mountains. In the New Brunswick forests there have been sightings of cougar, but their existence there has only recently been confirmed.

In New Brunswick, in 1894, the last sea mink was killed. This weasel, prized by trappers for its fur, was twice the size of the land mink. The species is now *extinct*.

All over the world various animals are in danger because of human activity. Their habitat may be destroyed as cities and farms expand, or pollution may upset their environment. Many different species of animals are now extinct. Others are endangered and, thankfully, people are becoming more concerned and aware about the threats of pollution and habitat destruction.

Two North American birds of prey, the Peregine Falcon and the Bald Eagle, were very close to extinction because of a pesticide called DDT. It worked its way up the food chain from the small insects it was meant to destroy to the falcons and eagles that preyed on the small, insect-eating birds. As a result, the eggs of the large birds had very soft shells which often broke, causing the babies to die. DDT was banned in 1972, and with a little help from biologists, both of these species are making a comeback.

What is the rarest animal in North America? The Black-footed Ferret was

> **Extinct:** no longer exists anywhere on earth
> **Extirpated:** doesn't exist in its former range
> **Endangered:** in serious danger of extinction or extirpation
> **Threatened:** likely to become endangered if factors affecting it are not altered.

threatened when its food source was destroyed. This large weasel preyed on prairie dogs. Prairie dogs were pests to farmers and were killed as thoroughly as possible. The ferrets lost their food source and died as well. In 1986, the few remaining ferrets were rounded up and bred in captivity. While some of them are being returned to the wild, they are still called "the rarest animal in North America."

What is the largest bird in Canada? The white Whooping Crane, at 1.4 meters long, is an *endangered* species. Its marshland habitat on the grasslands was drained to create farmland and the cranes lost their nesting sites. Around 1941, there were only 20 birds left in the wild. A law was passed to protect the Whooping Crane and scientists took measures to help nestlings survive. Now there are more than 200 cranes in the wild. They can be spotted in flight between their summer nesting ground at Wood Buffalo National Park in Alberta and their winter haven in Texas. The largest bird in Canada can be recognized in flight by its long, outstretched neck.

It is up to us to protect these animals and other endangered species in Canada and around the world.

Internet Links: Identify the silhouette of a flying Whooping Crane. See **Hinterland Who's Who**. Find out how scientists confirm the presence of cougars without seeing them. Go to Easylinks at **donnaward.net**

Lesson 36~Endangered Wildlife

1. Write the number showing why each animal became endangered or extinct.

_2_	Sea Mink	1.	Loss of food
_4_	Peregine Falcon	2.	Trapping
_1_	Black-footed Ferret	3.	Loss of habitat
_3_	Whooping Crane	4.	Pollution

2. Write the following terms beside the appropriate description.

    extinct   extirpated   endangered   threatened   vulnerable

    ___endangered___ The Vancouver Island marmot lives high in the mountains on Vancouver Island, hibernating in winter and eating grasses in summer. One of the rarest animals in the world, there are only about 100 of this species of marmot left alive today.

    ___extinct___ Funk Island, off the coast of Labrador, was once home to a flightless, penguin-like bird called the great auk. When George Cartwright visited the island in 1785, he wrote that hunters killing the bird for its feathers would soon destroy the whole breed. By 1845 great auks no longer existed.

    ___vulnerable___ The Atlantic cod was once the most valuable catch on the Grand Banks. While there are still millions of cod in the waters, they are smaller and fewer. The government put limits on the amount of cod which fishermen can catch, to prevent the species from becoming threatened or endangered.

    ___extirpated___ The great bison of the plains once sustained the Plains Natives, but was almost wiped out completely by the late 1800s. The only wild herd left in the world today resides in Wood Buffalo National Park located on the border which separates Alberta and the Northwest Territories.

    ___threatened___ The white beluga whale lives in arctic waters and a small group feed in the estuary of the St. Lawrence River. The beluga's melon-shaped forehead can collapse to create whistling sounds. Presently, population rates indicate a continuing decline.

Population

New Brunswick: 729,500
Fredericton: 47,560 (provincial capital)

Two Languages

New Brunswick, the only officially bilingual province, offers provincial services in both languages: schooling, policing, law courts and so on. Thirty-two percent of the population is of Acadian (French) descent. Moncton is the main city of the Acadian region. Fredericton and Saint John are primary locations for the English population.

New Brunswick's Two Families

Two families have had a profound impact on the economy of New Brunswick.

K.C. Irving began his career with an auto dealership. This led him into the garage business and gasoline sales, and eventually he became the owner of the largest oil refinery in Canada, a shipyard, and about 300 other companies. He bought newspapers, television and radio stations. After inheriting his father's lumber company in the 1930s, he began buying other lumber businesses. By the 1950s, he dominated the New Brunswick timber industry. With all these businesses you can imagine there are many New Brunswickers who earn their income with the Irving companies.

The other family is the McCains from Florenceville. Influenced by Mr. Irving, Harrison McCain, along with his brother Wallace, left their father's vegetable company and made a name for themselves in potato

History Highlights

	Micmac Natives hunt in land
1604	de Monts & Champlain build a settlement at St. Croix River
1713	Most of Acadia given to Britain & called Nova Scotia
1755	Acadians deported
1784	New Brunswick becomes a separate colony
1867	New Brunswick joins Dominion of Canada

processing. The popularity of french fries and the craze for fast-food restaurants in the 1950s gave them an open door. When New Brunswick potatoes were not as favoured for fries as the kind grown in warmer Idaho, U.S.A., the brothers were successful in developing a new potato which is now an industry standard. Building on their productivity, the McCains not only expanded internationally, but they bought up other food processing companies and diversified into many different products.

Unfortunately, disputes between the brothers led to a split and ugly court battles. Wallace and his sons left the McCain business and in 1995, bought Maple Leaf foods in Toronto.

Some New Brunswickers dislike how these two families own so many businesses. Others are glad for their enterprising spirit for it has brought much income to this province's economy.

Colour the population bar graph.
See library books on New Brunswick (adult & children's library section 917.15).
Also: Paul Waldie. *A House Divided: The Untold Story of the McCain Family.* (1996). (Adult).

NOVA SCOTIA CANADA'S OCEAN PLAYGROUND

Look at the art of the sea, how it shapes and polishes granite. Feel its cold cleanness; its power when it thunders against the land in a whole gale. If you stood on the rocks of Peggy's Cove on a day like this you would be in danger. . . . On fine days you can sit here in the sun with your back propped against North America and eyes ranging over a sea that extends uninterrupted to old (France) or (Africa).

Hugh Maclennan. *The Colour of Canada.*

(Toronto: McClelland & Stewart Ltd., 1967).

Nova Scotia is the Latin term for New Scotland. The Highlands of Nova Scotia reminded Scottish settlers of their home. Today, about thirty percent of Nova Scotians are of Scottish descent. Almost entirely surrounded by the sea, Nova Scotia has beautiful rocky caves, fishing hamlets and harbours. From boating on Cape Breton's saltwater lake, to whale watching at the mouth of the Bay of Fundy, Nova Scotia really is Canada's Ocean Playground.

Osprey

Far above the water an Osprey circles effortlessly. It may hover for an instant and then plunge like a dart straight down and into the water. In a few seconds it rises, scattering spray as it reaches for the air with a fish in its talons. A small fish may be devoured in flight, while a big catch will be carried to a favourite perch and eaten at leisure. Eagles will steal from Ospreys by pursuing them high in the sky until the exhausted Osprey drops its prey. Then the eagle swoops down to claim its prize. Ospreys mate for life, returning to the same nest year after year.

Mayflower

In spring, the Mayflower's scented pink blossoms bring colour to the woodlands.

Economics

In the past, Nova Scotians relied solely on their natural resources: fish, minerals and timber. As the number of resources dwindles, the people have to find new ways to earn a living. Manufacturing and tourism are two important areas of growth. The value of shellfish: lobster, snowcrab and mussels, has increased tremendously and this has brought a boom to the Nova Scotia fishery. Coal and offshore oil are important energy resources.

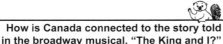

How is Canada connected to the story told in the broadway musical, "The King and I?"

The Anna Leonowens Art Gallery in Halifax is named after of a remarkable teacher who settled in Halifax and then in Montreal. Anna, born in Wales, married a British officer who was stationed in Singapore.

When her husband died, Anna and her young son journeyed to the dangerous country of Siam (Thailand) where, from 1862-67, she tutored the king's many children. She wrote two books; *The English Governess* and *The Romance of the Harem*. In 1943, M. Landon wrote Anna's biography, *Anna and the King of Siam,* which was the basis of the musical "The King and I," and the 1999 movie "Anna and the King."

Internet Links: Osprey Fact Sheet and photographs at **Hinterland Who's Who**. See **Government of Nova Scotia** Kids Site for Symbols and Bluenose Brainbuster Quiz. Easylinks at **donnaward.net**

Research and appropriately colour each symbol.

Mayflower

Osprey

Symbols of the Shield

(give the meanings of the symbols on the shield)

Cross of St. Andrew: _____

_____

Red Lion of Scotland: _____

_____

Shield

NOVA SCOTIA

Almost entirely surrounded by the ocean, Nova Scotia is affected by the sea in every area: the economy, the weather, the recreation. Wherever you are in Nova Scotia, the sea is less than 60 km away. From sculpted rocky inlets, to sandy beaches, to muddy tidal flats, Nova Scotia has an endless variety of seascapes. Both Cape Breton Island and the mainland lie in the *Appalachian Mountain Region.*

Winds, rain, and waves have hammered at Nova Scotia for centuries, wearing down the mountains and leaving breathtaking cliff views. There are two main land masses: the mainland peninsula and Cape Breton Island. Close to 4,000 islands nestle among the bays and inlets along the coast.

The rolling, rounded mountains, called the *Uplands,* are typical of the Appalachians. The Central Uplands are hilly and covered in pine and birch forests. Along the coast, they can be barren and rocky. On Cape Breton Island, the Uplands (also called *Highlands*) are too rugged for settlement, but their wild beauty attracts tourists. The Cabot Trail, one of the most well-known scenic drives in the world, follows the coastline in Cape Breton Highlands National Park and provides cliff-top views of the ocean, with twisting descents into small fishing hamlets.

As the hills slope toward the ocean, there is a narrow level strip of *Coastal Lowlands.* These lowlands contain the only productive farmland. The Annapolis Valley, famous for its fruit, lies between two upland regions close to the Bay of Fundy and is protected from the cold Fundy winds. Only 10% of Nova Scotia is fertile farmland.

The Bay of Fundy, which separates Nova Scotia and New Brunswick, boasts the world's highest tides. Because of the shape and size of the bay, the water can rise at high tide, up to 16 meters. The tide produces powerful tidal bores in the rivers, where the water is pushed opposite to the river current, sometimes in a notably sized wave. The bay waters are rich in nutritious food which attracts fish, whales, and seabirds.

Western winds carry weather from the continent into Nova Scotia. The presence of moist ocean air can produce fog, storms and much precipitation. The influence of the sea keeps Nova Scotia more moderate than the inland provinces, milder in winter and cooler in summer.

Who was Joseph Howe?

Joseph Howe (1804-1873), born in Halifax, had a passion for Nova Scotia and for integrity. He owned the newspaper the *Novascotian.* In 1835, he was charged for publishing an article denouncing local judges for poor practices. When no lawyer would defend him, he conducted his own defence and was acquitted triumphantly by the jury. His case confirmed freedom of the press in Canada.

In 1840, Howe's paper criticized another judge causing the judge's son to challenge Howe to a duel. The young man shot first and missed. Howe then fired into the air saying he would never deprive an old man of his only son. It is said of Howe that he was a man of great talent, courage, humour, and energy.

Who was Joshua Slocum?

Joshua Slocum was the first man to sail around the world alone. Originally from Annapolis, N.S., he went to sea at 16, and by the age of 25, he was a ship's captain. His wife lived aboard ship and his children were born at sea.

In 1894, at 50 years old, he bought an old boat and turned it into a seaworthy sail boat called the *Spray.* The Spray was 12 meters long.

In an incredible navigational feat, he sailed it around the world, taking just over 3 years. Slocum could not swim! He described his adventure in the book *Sailing Alone Around the World.*

In 1909 he set out in the *Spray* to sail to the Amazon River. He ran into a gale and neither he nor the Spray was ever seen again.

Using an atlas, mark the following places on the map below.

Halifax   Cape Breton Island
Truro   Bras d'Or Lake
Sydney   Strait of Canso
Digby

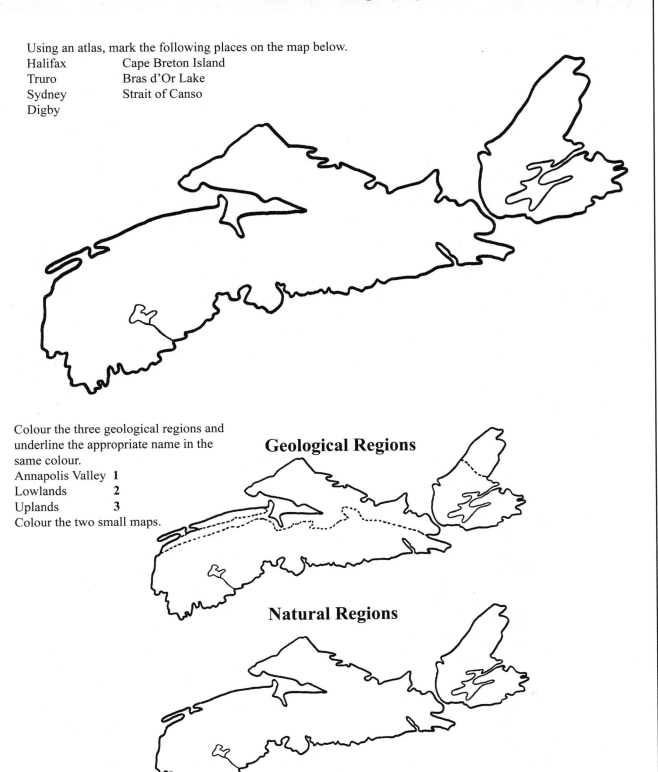

Colour the three geological regions and
underline the appropriate name in the
same colour.

Annapolis Valley **1**
Lowlands   **2**
Uplands   **3**

Colour the two small maps.

Geological Regions

Natural Regions

Fishing is the heartbeat of Nova Scotia. It has been said that while many Nova Scotians work in cities and would dread the thought of being on the waves in the biting wind, they are glad for the fishers who still do. The industry keeps alive the identity of the Nova Scotian.

Fishing is Canada's oldest industry. In the 1500s, fishing fleets from Europe summered in Newfoundland waters where they caught and dried codfish. The waters of the Canadian Atlantic were found to be teeming with fish. Why? The continental shelf along our east coast is a perfect fish habitat.

Sea plants need sunlight to grow, just like plants on land. Sunlight can penetrate the water to about 200 meters in depth. Where the ocean floor extends from the coast at this depth or less, it allows for much plant life and an abundance of food at the bottom of the food chain. As tiny plants develop, tiny animals feed on them. These microscopic plants and animals, called *plankton,* are eaten by small fish and crustaceans. They, in turn, become food for bigger fish. Large volumes of plankton mean lots of fish.

Where the ocean floor extends at 200 meters or less in depth, it is called the continental shelf. Raised areas are called banks. At Canada's Atlantic coast, the continental shelf extends a great distance before dropping off. This creates an excellent fish habitat. Many species of fish come to feed at the Grand Banks and the other banks around our Maritime provinces.

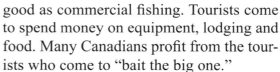

There are two types of fishing industries in Canada: *sport fishing* and *commercial fishing.* While in sport fishing, the fisherman is only hooking one fish at a time, the benefit to the economy can be almost as good as commercial fishing. Tourists come to spend money on equipment, lodging and food. Many Canadians profit from the tourists who come to "bait the big one."

In the commercial fishery, fishers with sophisticated boats and equipment challenge each other for the largest catch. Jobs are also created in fish processing plants and for equipment suppliers. Fluctuations in the fish numbers (stock) and changes in market prices create a very unsteady income for the fishers.

Canada does not sell much fish at home, but has to depend on markets in other countries. Why? Most Canadians live inland and they do not acquire a taste for fish like coastal dwellers, preferring meats such as beef, pork, and poultry. The commercial fishing industry depends on buyers outside of Canada.

In spite of our many lakes and long coastlines, only a few areas have enough fish

The Fish Food Chain

Mammals

Large Fish

Crustaceans, Small Fish

Plankton

to support commercial fishing. While some fishing is done on inland lakes or in the Arctic, the majority of fish is harvested on both the Pacific coast and to a greater extent, the Atlantic coast.

The offshore fishery is mainly comprised of the trawlers equipped with huge nets and freezers. They fish far out at sea remaining for two to three weeks. These large boats are not restricted by bad weather and are able to fish year round, twenty-four hours a day. The boats have sonar tracking equipment to find fish, rather than waiting for fish to enter their nets. The high cost of these boats makes them accessible only to large companies.

Fishers with small boats that stay closer to shore and return home each night, are called inshore fishers. Bad weather and the winter freeze often keep these fishermen off the waters. Inshore fishers complain that offshore trawlers make their catch before the fish reach the coast.

In recent years, the depletion of fish stocks has had a devastating effect on the Atlantic fisheries. The most important Newfoundland catch was cod. In the 1960's large trawlers began using dragnets that scooped up everything in their path. Sophisticated sonar equipment helped the ships find schools of fish, even when the stock was decreasing.

Inshore fishermen started sounding a warning when they noticed the cod on the Grand Banks were smaller and fewer than in the past. But by the time scientists and politicians realized how endangered the cod were, it was too late. Fish processing plants had to close and thousands of fishermen lost their livelihoods.

While Canadian officials control fishing within Canada's limit, offshore trawlers from other countries are not always dependable in practising good fish management, so this is a difficult battle.

> **What is the meaning of the name, Blomidon?** Blomidon, N.S., on the coast of the Minas Bay in the Bay of Fundy, is named from the nautical term "blow me down." This refers to a rushing wind coming down off a cliff which can topple and capsize a small sailing vessel.

Scientists continually research the decline in fish stocks to attempt a restoration and better stock management. Aquaculture, often called fish farming, may be one answer for the future. Fish bred and raised in controlled ponds mature quickly and safely. Fish management is certainly an area of importance if we hope to protect this resource for future generations.

Cape John, an offshore trawler, dwarfs the crabbing boats at the Louisbourg harbour, Cape Breton Island.

Canada's first English Thanksgiving service was celebrated at Port Royal, N.S. on October 9, 1710.

Lesson 40~Fishing

1.   About how many years have fishing fleets fished the waters of Newfoundland?

_____

2.   Match the definitions to the terms.

Food for small fish   raised area of the continental shelf
Continental shelf   plankton
Bank   up to 200 meters
Plankton   small fish
Food for large fish   ocean floor 200 meters or less
Sunlight penetrates water   microscopic plants and animals

3.   How does sport fishing benefit the economy?

_____

_____

4.   What two factors make it difficult for fishers to count on a steady income?

_____

_____

5.   Make at least three comparisons between offshore trawlers and inshore fishers.

Offshore	Inshore

Population

Nova Scotia: 908,007
Halifax Regional Municipality: 359,110

(provincial capital)

The Bluenose

The most legendary sailing ship in Canada's history, the Bluenose, was launched in Lunenburg, N.S. in 1921. Designed both as a fishing and a racing vessel, she was destined to win back the International Fisherman's Trophy lost to the Americans in 1920. In order to race, the ship and its crew had to have fished for one season on the Grand Banks. Commanded by Captain Angus Walters, the Bluenose defeated the Americans, won back the trophy and went on to win many races until its last in 1938.

Sold as a trading ship in 1942, the Bluenose hit a reef and sank near Haiti, only four years after the sale. The Bluenose is honoured with its profile on our 10 cent coin. Bluenose II, a replica built in the same shipyard in 1963, celebrates the grand days of the sailing ship and the victories of the Bluenose. It sails out of Halifax and Lunenburg, delighting tourists in the summer months.

Internet Links: See photographs of the Bluenose under sail at the **Official Site of Bluenose II**. See amateur crewman's videos of summer sailing. Easylinks at **donnaward.net**

History Highlights

	Micmac Natives dwell in the land
1605	Champlain & du Monts build Port Royal
1600's	French settlers emigrate to Acadia while France and Britain quarrel over land
1713	Nova Scotia (but not Cape Breton Island) given up to Britain
1719	French build Fort Louisbourg on Cape Breton Island
1755	British expel Acadians (French)
1758	Louisbourg falls to English
1867	Nova Scotia joins Dominion of Canada

Shellfish, Gold of the Sea

Once considered food only for the poor, lobster and other shellfish have become a delicacy in many nations. This fact has caused the market value to increase considerably. In an effort to control the number of fishers who harvest specific fish, the government stopped selling new licenses. Now they can only be passed on through the family, or bought from retiring fishers. Shellfish licenses sell at exorbitant prices. Coastguard patrols deal with the problem of shellfish poachers.

Colour the population bar graph.
See library books on Nova Scotia (adult & children's library section 917.16).
Also: Staebler, Edna. *Places I've Been and People I've Known.* **(1983, 1990).**
Michael Harris. *Lament for an Ocean: The Collapse of the Atlantic Cod Fishery.* **(1998). (Adult)**

PRINCE EDWARD ISLAND THE ISLAND

My discovery of Prince Edward Island began in June 1982. When I drove off the boat in Wood Islands. . . . through a countryside of green fields and blue coves rimmed by a red shoreline glowing orange in the evening light, I was spellbound. (God) must have created the Island in June, for in that month it's easy to believe that it is the most beautiful place on earth. The north shore harbours are bustling with activity of lobster season, purple lupins line the roadsides and, in the words of Lucy Maud Montgomery, "the greenness of everything is something to steep your soul in." I never got over that first encounter. So I moved to the Island and I've been here ever since.

John Sylvester. *From Red Clay and Salt Water.*
(Charlottetown: Ragweed Press, 1994).

Prince Edward was named to honour Queen Victoria's father, Prince Edward, Duke of Kent. The province's nicknames are *The Island, Garden of the Gulf,* and *Spud Island* after the fields of potatoes grown. The people of P.E.I. are proud of their island roots and call P.E.I. "The Island" as though no other island existed.

Blue Jay

Noisy and bossy, the Blue Jay shrieks out danger to other birds or dominates the backyard feeder. Its familiar scream of *jay jay jay* is combined with mimicry of other birds and is often heard in autumn when other birds are noticeably quiet. Jays are highly intelligent and bold, eating anything from seeds to insects, carrion (rotting meat) or fruit. Red Squirrels and Blue Jays may have a noisy war over a discovered cache of nuts hidden either by the jays or by the squirrels. The flash of blue over winter snow is a delight to many bird watchers.

Lady's Slipper

A type of orchid, the Lady's Slipper blossom looks like a tiny pink slipper. It loves damp, shady woodlands, and blooms in late spring.

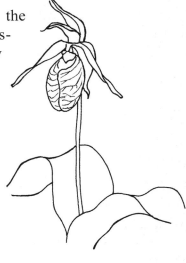

Economy

There are three important industries in P.E.I. The island's fertile soil and long growing season make it prime land for agriculture. The potatoe is one of the most important crops.

Attracted to the beaches and the quiet country life described in the world famous novel, *Anne of Green Gables*, visitors have made tourism the second most important industry in the province.

Finally, it seems obvious that fishing would be an important livelihood for many on the island. Lobsters and oysters are among the most valuable catches. Mussels are grown in protected bays under controlled conditions.

It's Bud the Spud,
from the bright red mud,
rollin' down the highway smilin'.
The spuds are big
on the back of Bud's rig;
They're from Prince Edward Island,
They're from Prince Edward Island.

Stompin' Tom Connors,
composer and singer
reproduced by Bob Davis in *Singin' About Us*
(Toronto: J. Lorimer,1976).

Internet Links: Blue Jay Fact Sheet with sound clips at and photographs at **Hinterland Who's Who** and also **Cornell Lab of Ornithology.** Easylinks at **donnaward.net**

93

Lesson 42~Symbols

Research and appropriately colour each symbol.

Lady's Slipper

Blue Jay

Symbols of the Shield
(give the meanings of the symbols on the shield)

Shield

Gold Lion: _____

_____

Oak Tree: _____

_____

Three Small Oak Trees: _____

_____

PRINCE EDWARD ISLAND

Prince Edward Island is predominantly *Lowland* with rich, rust-coloured soil. More than half of the island is farmland. The coastline includes long, sandy beaches, wind-carved sand dunes and low cliffs.

P.E.I. is separated from New Brunswick and Nova Scotia by the Northumberland Strait. The crescent shaped island is, at its widest, only 64 km. Most of the island consists of gently rolling hills, without the variations in landform that characterize the larger provinces. While it is part of the geological region called the *Appalachian Mountain Region*, the island is predominantly Lowland.

The vegetation of the island is that of the Mixed Wood Forest and is greatly influenced by the effects of the ocean in climate and precipitation. The island has been cleared almost completely for use as agricultural land. Since there are very few forested areas most of the large mammals are gone. Without many rivers or lakes the people rely on ground-water for their drinking supply. The colour of the soil, known worldwide for its rusty copper hue, is the result of iron oxide in the dirt that rusts when it is exposed to air. The red sandy shores are constantly changing by the force of the sea, eroding in some places, being built up by shifting sand in others. While the island has almost constant winds, the sea surrounding it keeps the temperature moderate.

"Sand dunes are the most fragile of habitats on Prince Edward Island. Our sand dunes are the areas of the province where we can most get the feeling of wilderness. . .The wind and the waves, or maybe the chirping of the birds is all you would hear. I can't think of anywhere else in this province that you can get such a feeling of wilderness." [1]

Internet Links: Travel on a virtual field trip with Natural Resources pilot, Dr. Ralph, at **Government of Nova Scotia**. Take an Atlantic Quiz. Easylinks **donnaward.net**

[1] John Sylvester. *From Red Clay & Salt Water.* (Charlottetown: Ragweed Pub., 1994), p. 18.

The beach at Cavendish is a favourite vacation playground.

Using an atlas, mark the following places on the map below.

Charlottetown	Hillsborough Bay
Summerside	Malpeque bay
Cavendish	
Souris	
Tignish	
West Point	

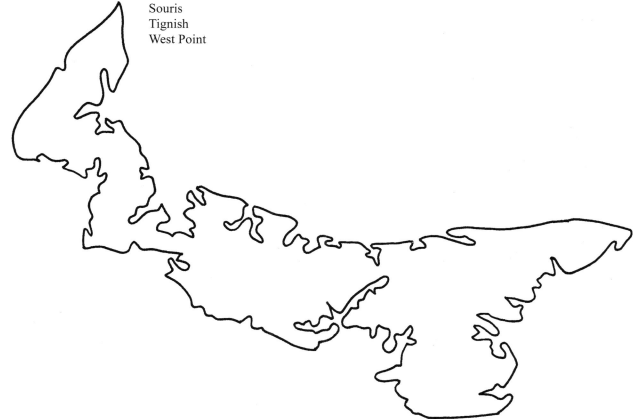

Natural Region: Mixed Wood Forest

Geological Region: Appalachian Mountain Region - Lowland

Tourism is one of Canada's fastest growing service industries. Business generated from both Canadian and foreign travellers provides jobs for more than 10% of working Canadians. Tourists spend their money on transportation, accommodation, food, recreation, and entertainment.

Not all visitors are on vacation. *Business travellers* contribute to half of the tourism income. At conferences and conventions, companies get together to share ideas or promote products. Businesses send representatives nationally and internationally to sell and buy goods, and to learn about new technology.

Canada's fantastic scenery and resources attract millions of *pleasure travellers* each year. The Rockies, Niagara Falls, and the Bay of Fundy are just a few of Canada's outstanding natural attractions. Popular recreations like downhill skiing, sport fishing, and canoe tripping thrill adventure seekers. Thousands each year are entertained by shows like *Anne of Green Gables* at Charlottetown and the *Calgary Stampede* in Alberta. Many advertising dollars are spent by each province in efforts to draw visitors to their locale. Canadians travelling within Canada account for about two-thirds of our travel income, though the number of foreign visitors increases yearly. Tourism is a big boost to the Canadian economy, but, until just recently, Canadians still spent more money travelling in other countries than the amount foreign visitors spent in Canada. Why is this travelling abroad not good for Canada's economy?

> Lucy Maud Montgomery's novels about Anne, the red haired orphan girl, are set in the idyllic countryside of Cavendish, P.E.I. Tourists flock by the thousands each summer to relive bits of the story. Visitors from Japan are especially enthralled with the "Anne" stories. Lucy Maud Montgomery once said to the Toronto Women's Press Club, "The critics condemn my books because of what they call my lack of realism. My reply to them is that sunsets are just as real as pigsties and I prefer writing about sunsets."[1]
>
> The popularity of Montgomery's stories has helped the tourist industry in P.E.I.

[1] Robert Colombo. *Colombo's 101 Canadian Place Names.* (Willowdale: Hounslow Press, 1983), p. 27.

Green Gables in Cavendish is an internationally known attraction.

Lesson 44~Tourism

1.   Tourists create jobs for Canadians by spending their money on what five things?

    _____

    _____

2.   What percentage of tourism income comes from business travellers?

    _____

3.   What kinds of things attract visitors to Canada?

    _____

    _____

4.   Explain why it is **not** good for the economy if Canadians spend more money travelling outside of Canada than within Canada.

    _____

    _____

    _____

5.   Name some places you would like to visit in Canada and tell why.

    _____

    _____

    _____

Population

Prince Edward Island: 135,294
Charlottetown: 32,245 (provincial capital)

Peter's Dream - by Lennie Gallant

I still get up before the day breaks.
I still walk down to the shore
I watch the sun rise from the eastern ocean,
But I don't sail to meet it any more.

How could they have let this happen
We saw it coming years ago
The greedy ships kept getting bigger and bigger
And the sonar told them where to go.

Chorus:
Last night I dreamed that I was sailing
Out on the sea of Galilee
We cast our nets upon the water
And Jesus pulled them in with me.

Where am I gonna go now
What about this boat I own
What about this old piano
What about my father's bones
Chorus

Someone sang an old sea shanty,
And Nealy told a mainland joke
Kelly cursed and swore until his voice gave out.
Then he asked me for a smoke.

Then he took his father's shotgun,
Walked to the harbour through the town
He fired fourteen times, woke everyone up. . .
And we all watched that boat go down.
Chorus

Lennie Gallant, from South Rustico, PEI, is a multiple East
Coast Music Award winner. Used with permission.
Questions for discussion:
Why don't the fishermen sail out any more?
Describe the mood portrayed in the third verse.
Why did Kelly do what he did?
What is the significance of the dream?

In the 1700s, Michel-Hache Gallant, Lennie Gallant's ancestor, is believed to be the first settler of European blood on the island. His father was French and his mother was native.

History Highlights

	Micmac aboriginals hunt in the land
1720	Acadians settle Port La Joye, name island Ile St-Jean
1755	Mainland Acadians escape deportation and come to island
1758	British take island from France & deport Acadians
1769	Island is separated from Nova Scotia
1799	Island is named Prince Edward Island
1864	Charlottetown Conference
1873	P.E.I. joins Confederation

Confederation Bridge

On May 31, 1997, amidst great fanfare, Confederation Bridge, a 12.9 km. long span of concrete, opened between P.E.I. and the mainland. Now, instead of waiting for the ferry, and spending 45-60 minutes crossing the Northumberland Strait, travellers can get to the island in 12 minutes.

Not only is this the longest bridge in the world to span ice-covered waters, but it also has to stand up to the extreme conditions of gale force winds, surging tides, and possible ship collisions.

Time will tell how this link to the mainland will change Prince Edward Island, but the boost it brings to the tourism industry is evident already.

Colour the population bar graph.
See library books on Prince Edward Island (adult & children's library section 917.17).
Also: Harry Thurston. *Building the Bridge to P.E.I.* (1998), Wayne Barrett and Anne MacKay. *Prince Edward Island, Red Soil, Blue Sea, Green Fields.* (1988), John Sylvester. *From Red Clay and Salt Water.* (1994).

NEWFOUNDLAND and LABRADOR THE ROCK

Oh, I loves the sea. I loves the sea. I understands the sea a lot. Now there is people afraid of the sea. I don't know why; they must have a reason. But me, I loves the sea.

Now you've got to respect the sea; you have to learn how to work together. If you don't feed yourself someone else has to do it. I did fish trapping, and I did fish trawling. Oh yeah, and jigging.

My dad and me would jig fish in shoal water. A steel hook, stuck into a big fish. Twenty pounds of wild fish, just five fathoms down. You haul in 150 of them, your hands wet and line slipping on your fingers.

Three thousand pounds for a dory, and maybe you would jig three boat-loads for a day. They were big fish then. They could eat the ones fisherman catch now. For lunch.

Lawrence Gibbons, retired fisherman, St. Vincent's, NFLD
Yva Momatiuk and John Eastcott, *This Marvellous Terrible Place.*
(Camden East: Camden House Pub., 1988).

The rocky rugged lands of Canada's most eastern province are known affectionately as "The Rock." Explorer John Cabot, first arriving at an unknown shore, called it "New Found Isle," but by 1502 it was being called "New found launde." Labrador comes from a Portuguese word meaning landowner. The constitutional name for the province was Newfoundland, however, the provincial government declared "Newfoundland and Labrador" the recognized name. In December, 2001, the federal government made "Newfoundland and Labrador" the official name.

Puffin

Puffins are social, maritime birds, which nest together on rocky cliffs and in crevices. The female lays a single egg. Both parents look after the youngster, bringing it fish until the colony breaks up in August. Puffins swim better than they fly, using their wings and their webbed feet to pursue small fish, especially caplin. They scoop up the fish and can hold many in their bill at one time. With a sharp decline in caplin, and harassment by gulls and man, Puffins are threatened. They are a protected species and cannot be hunted.

Pitcher Plant

Newfoundland's wet peat bogs are home to the insect-eating Pitcher Plant, the provincial flower. Its nectar attracts insects into its tube-shaped flower. The lining of downward-pointing bristles traps the bugs and the plant digests them.

Economy

The economy of Newfoundland and Labrador has always been tied almost completely to the resources of the sea. The most important fish was cod. In recent years however, the cod stock has become so depleted that the people have had to find new ways of earning an income. The large offshore Hibernia oil well, and the recent development of a large nickel mine will be a boost to a struggling economy.

Internet Links: Puffin Fact Sheet with sound clips and photographs at **Cornell Lab of Ornithology.** Easylinks at **donnaward.net**

Research and appropriately colour each symbol.

Pitcher Plant

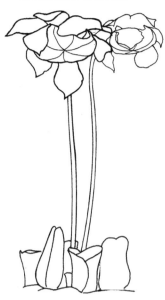

Puffin

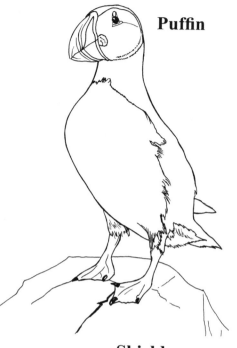

Symbols of the Shield

(give the meanings of the symbols on the shield)

Shield

Silver Cross:_____

_____

Lions:_____

_____

Unicorns: _____

_____

NEWFOUNDLAND and LABRADOR

Newfoundland and Labrador are two distinct tracts of land but they are one province. Labrador is the mainland area which lies in the region of the *Canadian Shield*. The island of Newfoundland is part of the *Appalachian Mountain* region. Both have rugged, rocky coastlines with many deep fjords and inlets.

On the island of Newfoundland, the Long Range Mountains stretch up the west coast, dropping steeply into the Gulf of St. Lawrence. Inland, the rolling plateau is covered with shallow, rocky soil so that only spruce, pine, and fir survive. Newfoundland's southern and eastern coasts are lower-lying, yet they are still rugged with crags and steep cliffs.

The Avalon Peninsula, connected to the rest of the island by a narrow strip of land, boasts St. John's, the most easterly city in North America. Experts from Environment Canada have stated that the people of St. John's experience the most severe weather in Canada. They have the wettest, windiest, foggiest, cloudiest, and snowiest days of the year.

On the mainland, the rugged Torngat Mountains in Labrador's far north are beautiful but barren, with rivers that carve out rock on their race to the sea. The north half of the mainland is in the treeless Taiga Shield, where caribou roam the moss covered, rocky land. Only shrub trees survive the harsh climate. South, to the coast, the Boreal Shield is a wild land of spruce forests, rocky outcrops, and bogs.

The weather is affected by ocean currents. The Labrador current brings arctic water along the mainland coast, which keeps the weather quite cold. A sure sign of spring is the appearance of icebergs which float down from Greenland. They sometimes last months stuck on an underwater shoal before melting. The warmer waters of the Gulf Stream, flowing by Newfoundland, keep the island about five degrees warmer than Labrador.

Internet Links: See photo gallery at **Our Labrador.** Under Communities, Southern Labrador, I especially enjoyed photographs of Williams Harbour and Mary's Harbour. For these and more links go to Easylinks at **donnaward.net**

How many icebergs pass Newfoundland?

The International Ice Patrol was formed in 1914, two years after the sinking of the Titanic. Founded by 19 nations, its job is to monitor the movements of all icebergs sighted below the 59th parallel, just south of Labrador. They estimate that about 400 icebergs leave Greenland glaciers each year and drift past Newfoundland. Once they enter the warm waters of the Gulf Stream they melt within about two weeks.

Lobster fishing is an important part of the fishing industry in Newfoundland.

Lesson 47~Geography

Geological Regions

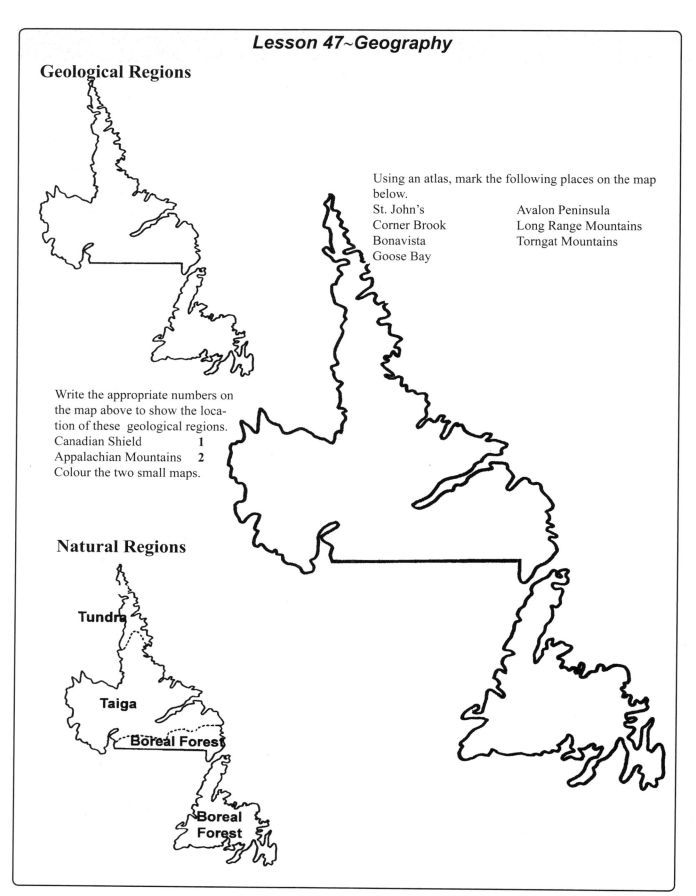

Using an atlas, mark the following places on the map below.

St. John's   Avalon Peninsula
Corner Brook   Long Range Mountains
Bonavista   Torngat Mountains
Goose Bay

Write the appropriate numbers on the map above to show the location of these geological regions.

Canadian Shield   **1**
Appalachian Mountains   **2**
Colour the two small maps.

Natural Regions

Tundra

Taiga

Boreal Forest

Boreal Forest

Trains, dishwashers, copper pipes, nails, nylon clothing, bicycles, and door knobs– what do these things have in common? They are all made from some form of mineral.

Have you ever gathered coloured pebbles at the seashore, or walked along a rocky outcrop and noticed the different colours in the rock? The colours come from the minerals which make up the rock. When high concentrations of a useful mineral are found, they can be mined for human use. The rock is referred to as *ore*. Minerals are a non-renewable resource; once removed, they are gone forever.

Minerals can be grouped into metallics, non-metallics and fossil fuels.

Metallics

Precious metals, such as gold and silver, and *base metals* like iron, zinc, and copper are found in igneous rock in the Canadian Shield. These metals are usually shiny, hard, and in processing, easy to shape. When they are mixed with other metals, they are called *alloys*. Iron for instance, used to make steel, can be mixed with other minerals such as nickel to make it harder or rust resistant.

Non-Metallics

Nonmetallics are lighter in colour and weight, with a duller lustre. Nonmetallic minerals have different uses. Potash is used in plant fertilizer. Asbestos is a threadlike mineral which can be woven into fire resistant cloth or added to cement to strengthen it. Quartz and salt are also nonmetallic minerals.

Structural minerals are non-metallics used in the construction of roads and build-ings. Cement is made from a mixture of lime and other minerals. When mixed with sand, gravel and water, it can be made into concrete for highways and buildings. Sand and gravel, called *aggregate*, are mined from all types of rock. Most construction sites are close to a supply of aggregate.

Types of Mining

Of the two types of mining, *open-pit* mining is the least expensive. This method involves blasting the rock with explosives and then hauling the ore out with power shovels and trucks to the processing plants. Most of Canada's iron ore is mined this way. The problem with this type of mining is the huge hole left in the landscape when the ore deposits are all removed. Although it is expensive, sites in settled areas are often restored by returning waste rock to the pit, covering it with soil, and replanting with grass or trees. In remote areas, mining companies do not usually restore the sites. The second method, *underground* mining, is more expensive because of the drilling and safety structures required to access ores deep within the earth's surface. Mining engineers must plan for underground pumps, air ventilation and other methods to keep the mine safe for workers.

Bay of Hope or Bay of Despair?

On the south coast of Newfoundland lies a little port which was called by the French in the 17th century, "Baie d'Espoir," which means "Bay of Hope." The name today is spelled almost the same, "Bay d'Espoir," but the pronunciation is English, "Bay Despair." This is the fishing community that went from *hope* to *despair* in three centuries.

Lesson 48~Mining

1.   Rock that contains high concentrations of a useful mineral is called?

_____

2.   What are the three groupings of minerals?

_____

3.   Match the terms.

Precious metals   mixed metals
Base metals   materials used in construction
Alloy   sand and gravel
Nonmetallic minerals   gold and silver
Structural minerals   quartz and salt
Aggregate   iron, zinc and copper

4.   Why is underground mining more expensive than open-pit mining?

_____

_____

_____

5.   In what areas do mining companies restore open-pit sites?

_____

_____

Population

Newfoundland and Labrador: 512,930
St. John's: 172,918 (provincial capital)

Newfoundland Dialect

Isolation from the rest of Canada and the strong legacy of Scottish and Irish roots has produced dialects different from any other part of the country. Accents vary from one local region to another.

Guess what some of these sentences mean.

My throat is so sore I can't glutch anything.
When the cousins come, the house is in a reeraw;
        so, we all have to help with the clobber.
It's hard to get the boat across the slobby.
We were dodgin' along, enjoying the sun.
You sure can fadge for yerself now, b'y.
It's a mauzy old day, sir.
Boy, 'tis fafferin' today.
Clean up! You're slommocky!
What are you gatching about tonight?
The kids are sleeping. Not a joog in any of 'em. [1]

b'y:	boy, term of address for all males, except the father or master
clobber:	untidy, cluttered from activity
dodging:	strolling casually, leisurely
fadge:	manage on one's own
faffering:	wind blowing in cold, chilly gusts
gatch:	show-off, boastful manner
glutch:	swallow
joog or jook:	sign of life, or energy
mauzy:	damp, foggy, misty, light rain, cool gentle wind off the sea.
reeraw:	disorder, hulabaloo
slobby:	dense, slushy mass of ice bits
slommocky:	slovenly, untidy appearance

Internet Links: More interesting NFLD words at **Word Play.** Also see **Word Play** for interesting NFLD place names. See photos of the Hibernia Oilfield at **Hibernia.** For these and more links go to Easylinks at **donnaward. net**

History Highlights

Woodland hunting aboriginals and coastal Inuit live in the land.

1000	Vikings build a settlement at L'Anse aux Meadows
1497	John Cabot harbours at St. John's
1881	Building of a railway begins on the island
1892	Much of St. John's is destroyed by fire
1927	Newfoundland and mainland Labrador are joined
1947	Newfoundland becomes the tenth province in Canada

Sporting Dogs

Two dog breeds originated in this province: Labrador Retrievers and Newfoundland dogs. Large and strong, with good temperaments, their webbed feet make them excellent swimmers. They are used by hunters to retrieve game and by rescuers to save drowning victims. The "Labs" can be black, pale gold, or chocolate coloured with short, sleek hair. The "Newfs" have heavy black, or black and white coats with long, shaggy hair.

[1] Dictionary of Newfoundland English. (Toronto: University of Toronto Press, 1989).

Colour the population bar graph.
See library books on Newfoundland and Labrador (adult & children's library section 917.18).
Also: Yva Momatiuk. *This Marvellous Terrible Place, Images of Newfoundland and Labrador.* **(1988).**
G.M. Story, W.J. Kirwin, J.D.A. Widdowson (ed). *Dictionary of Newfoundland English.* **(1982).**

YUKON
LAND OF THE
MIDNIGHT SUN

There's a land where the mountains are nameless,
And the rivers all run God knows where;
There are lives that are erring and aimless,
And deaths that just hang by a hair.
There are hardships that nobody reckons;
There are valleys unpeopled and still;
There's a land - oh, it beckons and beckons,
And I want to go back - and I will.

There's gold, and it's haunting and haunting;
It's luring me on as of old
Yet it isn't the gold that I'm wanting
So much as just finding the gold.
It's the great, big, broad land 'way up yonder,
It's the forests where silence has lease,
It's the beauty that thrills me with wonder,
It's the stillness that fills me with peace.

Robert Service. "The Spell of the Yukon."
(first published in 1907).

The Yukon River, the second-longest river in Canada, starts in the mountains of northern B.C., flows through the Yukon into Alaska, and empties into the Bering Sea. It has always been a travelway for Native peoples and gold seekers. The name came from the Native Kutchin word meaning "great river." The territory adopted this name, expressing how important the river has been in the lives of the people of the Yukon.

On the longest day of the year, June 21st, the sun never fully sets in the far north. In Old Crow, the sun dips to the horizon and then starts to rise again. Dawson City sees 21 hours of sunlight and Whitehorse, 19 hours. For this reason it is called the "Land of the Midnight Sun." On December 21st, Old Crow residents see no sun at all; Dawson City has only about 4 hours, and Whitehorse, just 5.5 hours of daylight at this time.

Common Raven

The Common Raven is the largest member of the crow family. It is completely black, including its beak and feet. While it prefers mountains and coasts, it can be found almost anywhere in Canada. In the north, the raven population is high.

A favourite figure in many native legends, the raven has both positive and unique features. As a scavenger, it is part of nature's cleanup crew, feeding on animal carcasses and garbage. One way the Common Raven can be distinguished from its relative, the crow, is the fact that unlike the crow, it has to take a few hops before launching into flight. Though not very colourful, the raven is an important part of the bird community.

Internet Links: Fact Sheet with sound clips of the Common Raven at **Cornell Lab of Ornithology.** Find out how sour dough works, and try making it yourself. See **How Stuff Works.** For these and more links go to Easylinks at **donnaward.net**

Fireweed

The Fireweed is the first plant to grow in the open spaces after a forest fire. It flowers all summer in purplish-red blossoms which open from the base of a cluster upwards. Each bloom lasts only two days. Both moose and cattle feed on the Fireweed. The new shoots can be cooked and eaten like asparagus.

Economy

Since there is very little farming or manufacturing in the Yukon, the economy is based on mining, tourism, and government jobs. As in every region, the service industry is also an important area of employment.

What is a sourdough?

Miners during the Klondike Gold Rush found that sourdough bread was a practical food supply. Veteran prospectors were nicknamed 'sourdoughs.'

Lesson 50~Symbols

Research and appropriately colour each symbol.

Fireweed

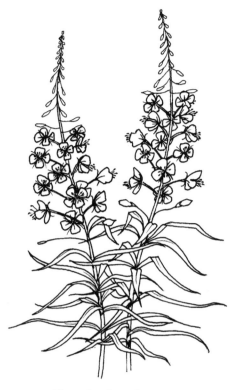

Common Raven

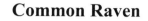

Symbols of the Shield

(give the meanings of the symbols on the shield)

Cross of St. George:

_____

Wavy White Stripes:

_____

Red Peaks & Gold Discs:

_____

Shield

YUKON

The tail end of the *Western Cordillera* extends into the Yukon in a series of mountain ranges, plateaus and river valleys. The highest mountain in Canada, Mount Logan, in the St. Elias Range, is 5959 metres high.

The most spectacular mountains in the Yukon are the St. Elias Mountains, a continuation of the B.C. Coast Mountains. They cut through the southwestern part of the territory and continue on into Alaska. They are snow-covered year round and contain many glaciers. Kluane National Park preserves this remote, untamed wilderness for the growing number of adventure seekers looking for wild lands.

The interior mountains are an extension of the Rockies. The south-central ranges are the Pelly Mountains. Straddling the Northwest Territories/Yukon border are the Mackenzie Mountains with the Selwyn Range on the Yukon side.

The Yukon River and its tributaries have carved river valleys through the plateau and mountain area. The Yukon River is generally wide and has become a favourite canoe route for trippers following the historical trail of the gold seekers of the 1897-98 Klondike Stampede. White water enthusiasts enjoy the many other fastwater rivers which run from the mountains throughout the Yukon.

The treeline crosses the territory diagonally almost at the middle point, separating the Tundra from the Boreal forest. The permafrost makes it impossible for trees to grow in the northern regions.

Old Crow, the Yukon's most northerly community, is 130 km north of the Arctic Circle. The population of about 200 Natives have access to the outside world by air travel only, as it is the only settlement in the Yukon not connected by a highway.

Yukon Gold!

George Carmack, from California, was twenty-five when he headed north to the Yukon in 1885. He married a Tagish Native woman and prospected for gold with two of her brothers. Eleven years later, they discovered gold nuggets in a creek near Dawson. It was not long before news of the gold strike travelled around the world. That was the beginning of the Klondike Gold Rush, which changed the face of the Yukon forever.

Mining is still important in the Yukon, although high operating costs and low sale prices on the world market have caused many mines in the territory to close.

Internet Links: Yukon Quiz at **Fun Trivia**. Go to Easylinks at **donnaward.net**

"What is a Yukoner?" - Anonymous

With something like 20,000 people sharing 207,076 square miles, maybe it's the space or freedom that makes the real Yukoner tick. His love for his country is inarticulate-he can seldom explain it and would be embarrassed to try. He puts up with atrocious weather during the year. He often does without the amenities of modern civilization. He grumbles about the lack of green grass, the slowness of development and the indifference of the rest of Canada. But deep down, he hugs a secret-a certainty that when all things are tallied, he comes out way ahead.

He knows his country is more beautiful, more unspoiled than any other and his history more exciting. His sense of humour is mischievous and good naturedly directed against those from Outside. His clannishness with other Yukoners in the Outside world is phenomenal. His energy in undertaking anything he does is tremendous. His impatience with senseless regulations can get him into trouble. Unawed by visiting celebrities, skeptical of experts, contemptuous of phonies- he is helpful to newcomers, fond of eccentrics and he never worries about his own "identity" because he's got it - he's a Yukoner.

Yukon Sourdough Rendezvous Booklet (The Whitehorse Star, 1968).

Colour the two maps.

Geological Regions
The Yukon lies in the Western
Cordillera region

Using an atlas, mark the follow-
ing places on the map below.
  Whitehorse
  Dawson
  Old Crow
  Yukon River
  Lake Laberge
  Porcupine River
  Peel River
  Mount Logan

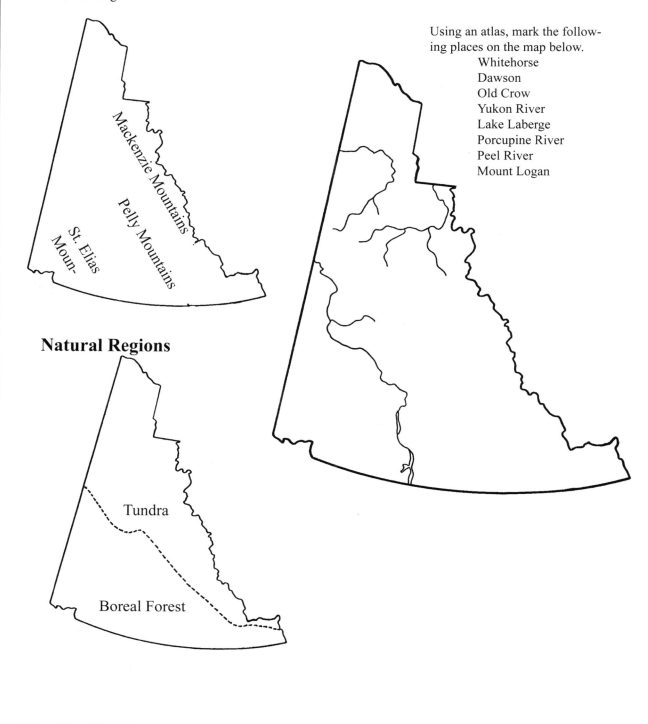

Mackenzie Mountains

Pelly Mountains

St. Elias
Moun-

Natural Regions

Tundra

Boreal Forest

Population

Yukon Territory:	28,674
Whitehorse:	23,205 (territorial capital)
Dawson:	2,020

The Man Who Told the Klondike Tales

The thrill of the Klondike: the wild adventure and the unbearable trail, sled dogs and ice-covered whiskers, restless miners and the Mounted Police! No one has captured it better than the young banker who experienced the tail end of the gold rush first hand.

Wanderlust led young Robert Service to the Canadian west and then, in 1904, to the Yukon where he saw the last days of the 1897-98 gold stampede. As miners recounted outlandish tales, Service brilliantly captured them in the poetry that seized the attention of the English speaking world. His most famous ballad was "The Cremation of Sam McGee." The popularity of his writing allowed him to quit his job as a bank teller and begin writing full-time.

Just before the First World War, in 1912, Service left the Yukon for good to become a European correspondent for the Toronto Star. After marrying a French girl in 1913, he permanently settled in France. Robert Service was more a gentleman of leisure than the roughneck described in his books. He loved travelling to exotic places.

Though he wrote many stories and poems over the years, Service's fame still rests on the colourful ballads of Klondike days in the Yukon.

History Highlights

	Native peoples dwell in the land
1842	Fort Frances is built by the Hudson's Bay Company
1895	North West Mounted Police bring law and order to the Yukon
1896	Gold is found near Dawson City
1897	Klondike Gold Rush begins
1898	The Yukon is divided from the North-West Territory, becoming a separate territory
1942	Construction of the Alaskan highway begins
1953	The Yukon capital is moved from Dawson City to Whitehorse

The Northern Lights

Shimmering, shifting ribbons of colour: green, pink, and blue, dance in the night sky. The northern lights, or "aurora borealis" can be seen on clear nights in the north, especially in late fall and early spring. Electrically charged particles blown in from the sun contact gases (oxygen and nitrogen) in our atmosphere and begin to glow like neon lights in a phenomenal display.

What is Canada's deepest body of water?

Great Slave Lake in the Northwest Territories is the deepest body of water in Canada. At 614 metres deep, it would cover the CN Tower in Toronto, which is 553 metres high.

Colour the population bar graph.
See library books on the Yukon (adult & children's library section 917.12).
Also: Ken Madsen. *Wild Rivers, Wild Lands*. (1996).

NORTHWEST TERRITORIES LAND OF THE PEOPLE

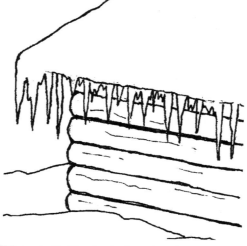

Winter in the Territories lasts from September to June.

Little Lady Icicle is dreaming in the north-land
Gleaming in the north-land, her pillow all a-glow
For the frost has come and found her
With an ermine robe around her
Where little Lady-Icicle lies dreaming in the snow.

Little Lady Icicle is waking in the north-land,
and shaking in the north-land her pillow to and fro;
And the hurricane a-skirling
Sends the feathers all a-shirling
Where little Lady Icicle is waking in the snow.

Johnson, E. Pauline. "Lady Icicle," Flint and Feather .
(first published in 1912).

The Northwest Territories originated as a place name referring to most of western and northern Canada. As provinces were formed, its border became established. In April, 1999, the vast land was divided into two territories: Nunavut in the northeast, and the remaining Northwest Territories in the west. The native Dene people, whose home has been along the Mackenzie River, call their land Denendeh which means "land of the people."

Gyrfalcon

The Gyrfalcon, the largest of the falcons, lives on the tundra. Similar to a hawk, the falcon differs by its long pointed wings, long tail, and different flight patterns. Rather than soar, falcons flap rapidly and swoop down on their prey from above, grabbing it by the throat with long, strong talons.

Mountain Avens

The small, white Mountain Avens carpets the ground in July. On each stem, a single white flower with a yellow centre pokes up toward the sun. The flowers turn to face the sun as the earth rotates. The Mountain Avens is a member of the rose family.

Who invented the snowmobile?

Armand Bombardier designed the skidoo around 1922 and began manufacturing it in 1959. Prior to that, in 1898, a Quebec City dentist, Dr. H. Edmond Casgrain, put together a winter carriage with two front steel runners and a single back wheel with a studded tire that could drive through ice and snow.

Internet Links: Fact Sheet with sound clips Gyrfalcon at **Cornell Lab of Ornithology.** Look at **CBC archives** about the Bombardier company. For these and more links go to Easylinks at **donnaward.net**

Economy

Mining is the most important industry in the Northwest Territories, with gold being mined near Yellowknife. In 1991, diamonds were discovered near Lac de Grass, northeast of Yellowknife. The site, which opened in the fall of 1998, provides hundreds of jobs. Along with mining: government jobs, tourism, and the sale of Native Dene crafts bring health to the economy.

Lesson 53~Symbols

Research and appropriately colour each symbol.

Mountain Avens

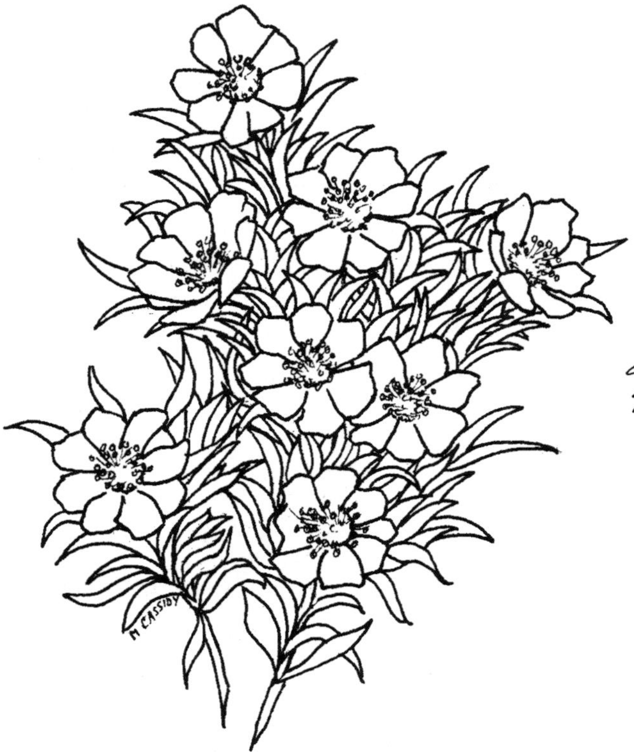

Gyrafalcon

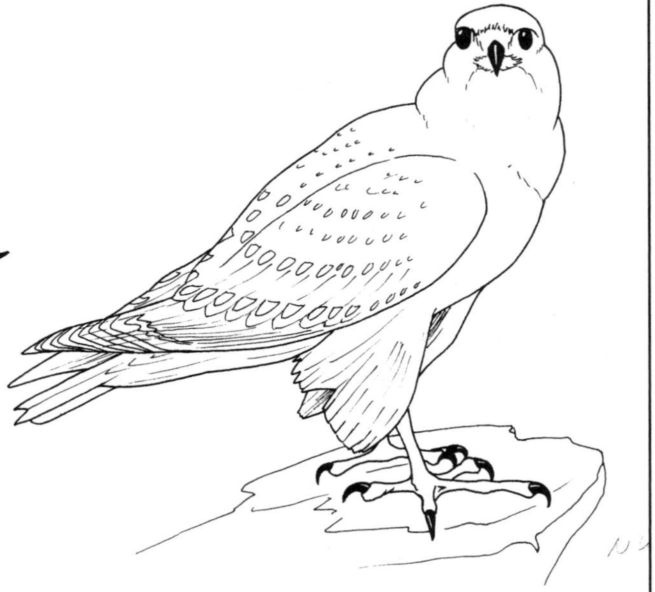

Shield

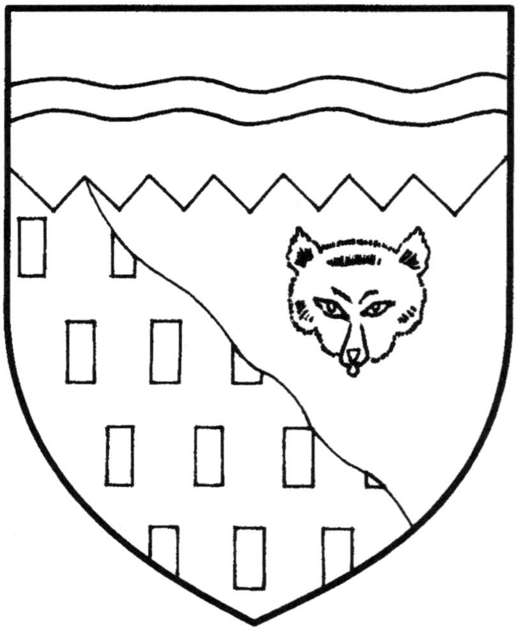

Symbols of the Shield

(give the meanings of the symbols on the shield)

Blue Wavy Line Over White: ____________________

____

Gold Bars on Green: ____________________

____

White Fox on Red: ____________________________

____

Northwest Territories

The Northwest Territories is comprised of each of the three main geological regions. The tail end of the *Western Cordillera* separates the Northwest Territories and the Yukon. The *Interior Plains* stretch up along the Mackenzie River and, to the east of the territory, the *Canadian Shield*

The Mackenzie Mountains of the *Western Cordillera* have deep river canyons, grassy sinkholes and rocky caves. Much of this wild terrain is yet unexplored.

The *Interior Plains* contain the Mackenzie River, Canada's longest, which starts at Great Slave Lake and empties into the Arctic Ocean. At its mouth, the Mackenzie River delta is one of the largest in the world, 80 kilometers across. Deposits of mud and sand have created many islands and channels. The Plain holds deposits of oil and natural gas.

The western part of the *Canadian Shield* begins near Yellowknife, and stretches east into Nunavut. Since the border between these two territories basically follows the treeline, much of the Northwest Territories is in the Natural regions of *Taiga Shield* or *Taiga Plain*.

The Mackenzie River Valley provides the only area sheltered enough for pine and spruce to survive. The valley receives the most precipitation of the north, yet even that is limited, to about 38 cm per year. The warmest northern temperatures are around Great Slave Lake and Yellowknife where the bulk of the population dwells.

Sinkholes

When water dissolves limestone, creating an underground cavern, the land above eventually collapses, forming a sinkhole. Many sinkholes exist in the north.

Bush Planes

Adventuresome Canadian pilots perfected the skill of 'bush flying' in Canada's northland. The countless waterways offered landing spots for planes on floats or on skis in winter. Extreme weather conditions, remote wilderness and primitive aeroplanes made it dangerous for pilots.

Bush pilots were first hired by forest companies who wanted them to spot forest fires. Then they began to be used by mining companies. One of the longest flights was achieved by pilot Leigh Brintnell. In 1929, he dropped the prospector Gilbert LaBine at Great Bear Lake, flew on to Aklavik on the Arctic coast, went to Edmonton and then back to Winnipeg. The trip totalled 15,000 km. In the meantime, at Great Bear Lake, LaBine found radium and struck it rich.

Bush planes became a form of transportation for trappers, missionaries, prospectors and people in need of medical attention.

Today, many remote centers have an airstrip for conventional small planes. Air travel remains the most effective transportation in the north.

Internet Links: See photographs of Cambridge Bay, NWT and other information on the Kiilinik High School's community atlas. Go to Easylinks at **donnaward.net**

Lesson 54~Geography

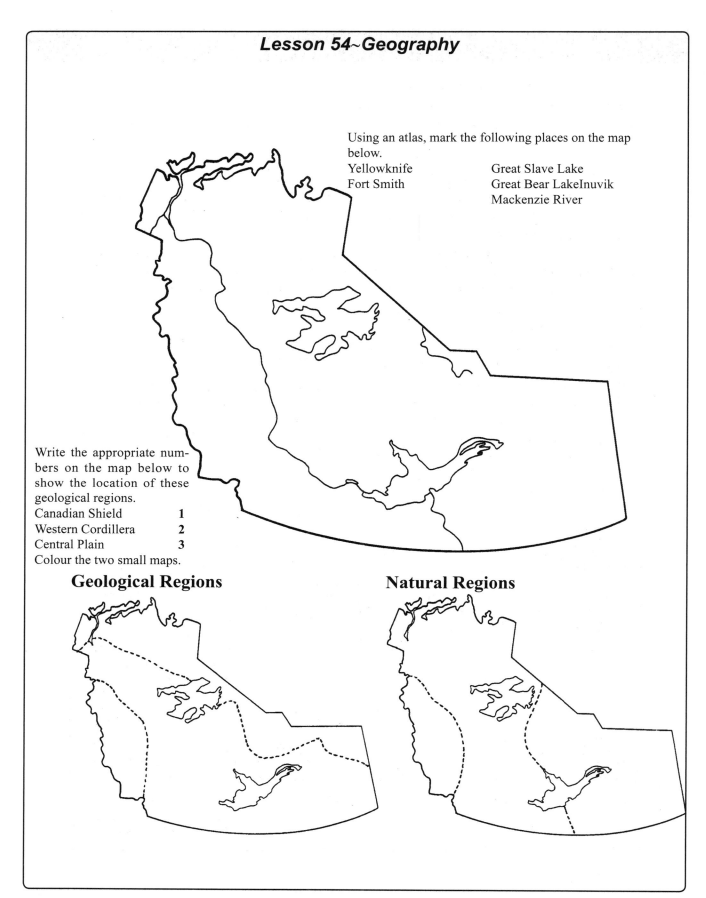

Using an atlas, mark the following places on the map below.

Yellowknife
Fort Smith

Great Slave Lake
Great Bear LakeInuvik
Mackenzie River

Write the appropriate numbers on the map below to show the location of these geological regions.

Canadian Shield   **1**
Western Cordillera   **2**
Central Plain   **3**
Colour the two small maps.

Geological Regions

Natural Regions

Population

Northwest Territories: 37,360
Yellowknife: 20,000 (territorial capital)

Canada's First Diamond Mine

Northwest Territories, dependent on gold mining and the government, is benefiting from the Ekati Diamond Mine which opened in October 1998. In an area of high unemployment the 2000 jobs are a big boost to the economy. The mine produces 6% of the world's diamonds.

Since safeguarding the environment is a top priority to today's generation, the mine is required to pay $450,000 per year to a "watch-dog" agency who will make sure that the fragile Arctic environment is protected. Before the mine was allowed to open, studies had to be made on the possible effects of the mine on the bird life, water quality, migrations of the caribou and on the endangered Barren Grounds Grizzly Bear.

With other diamond mines opening in the north, there has been an outcry that the tundra and its animal population is at risk.

Internet Links: Look for links about diamond mining at Easylinks - **donnaward.net**

The Arctic is lifeless, except for millions of caribou and foxes, tens of thousands of wolves and musk oxen, thousands of polar bears, millions of birds, and billions of insects.

Vilhjalmur Stefansson, Arctic explorer, quoted by Fred Bruemmer in *The Arctic*, 1974.

History Highlights

	Indigenous people dwell in the land
1670	Prince Rupert's Land is given to the Hudson's Bay Company
1789	Alexander Mackenzie looks for a western passage and canoes down the Mackenzie River
1870	Prince Rupert's Land and the North-western Territory are joined
1933	Gold discoveries boost the population of Yellowknife
1967	Yellowknife becomes the capital of NWT
1982	Residents of NWT agree to divide territory into two
1999	New territory of Nunavut is formed from the northeast section of Northwest Territories

The Last Frontier

The north is no paradise. If it were, more people would be living there. The north has one basic flaw; winter dominates its year. . . . cold is the north's burden. Most people, and most birds in the north, are part-time users, enjoying the summer but retreating from the winter. In spite of the harshness of the northern landscapes and of the problems that the animals must surmount, there is an abundance of animal life to see. . . . Much of Canada is still wild country, and much of that wildness is the result of the land having severe limitations for traditional human use. . . .Where there is wildness . . . . (there) will be clean water, clean air, space, solitude freedom.

[1] R. Yorke Edwards, "The Proof of Wildness: Where Caribou Still Stand," Borden Spears (ed) *Wilderness Canada,* (Toronto: Clarke, Irwin & Company Ltd..,1970).

Colour the population bar graph.
See library books on the Northwest Territories (adult & children's library section 917.12).

NUNAVUT OUR LAND

My name is Marion Tuu'laq. One time, while we were at Tipyalik, there were no caribou to be found, and we became very hungry. We didn't even see any caribou tracks. We were forced to live on dog meat. Killing and eating our dogs was the only way we could survive. After we no longer had any dogs, we packed all our belongings on our backs, and we started to walk. I don't know how many days we had wandered and nights we had slept before we reached our igloo.

We had not had anything to eat for a long time, and we were very thin and nearly starved to death. Then Nattaq and others who had killed some caribou, came to our igloo. That night, after all of us had eaten our fill, we started to tell stories. As usual, I found lots to laugh at. In those days, I used to laugh often. Now, everything seemed so funny. When Nattaq started to talk again about how she thought I might be dead, I started to laugh. "This girl never runs out of laughs," my brother, Angutituaq, said.

Excerpts of a true story in "A Story of Starvation."
Robin Gedalof (ed.), *Paper Stays Put, A Collection of Inuit Writing.*
(Edmonton: Hurtig Publishers Ltd., 1980).

The new eastern territory called Nunavut (Noon-a-vut) means "our land." It was created as a division from the Northwest Territories on April 1, 1999. This is the first Canadian region governed by indigenous people. Eighty-five percent of the residents are Inuit, with more than half of them younger than 25 years of age.

Economy

A large percentage of the Inuit population still relies on traditional hunting and fishing. Many of the wage earners work for the government. Inuit carvings and art work are becoming famous around the world and are a valuable source of income. Tourism is also a developing business as southerners are drawn to the solitude and stark beauty of this unexplored wilderness.

With almost every mineral present in the rock of the Shield, mining could be a chief source of income, however, high production costs and low market prices have discouraged extensive mining.

Inuktitut

The traditional language of the Inuit, Inuktitut, is spoken by more than 70% of the population in Nunavut. It is a compulsory subject in school for children from kindergarten to grade four. Nunavut has three official languages: French, English and Inuktitut.

Who are called "snowbirds"?
Who are called "ducks"?
"Snowbirds" are Canadians who flee the snow by living part of each winter in the sunny southern states. Summer visitors to the Arctic are called "Ducks."

Coat of Arms

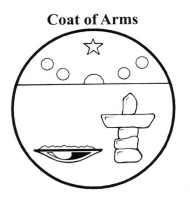

In the right base of the shield in the Nunavut coat of arms, the inuksuk symbolizes the stone monuments which guide the people on the land and mark sacred places. The inuksuk is blue on a yellow background.

The qulliq, or Inuit stone lamp, represents light and the warmth of family and the community. It is black at the base and red on the top, against a yellow background.

Above, the concave arc of five gold circles on a blue background, refers to the life-giving properties of the sun arching above and below the horizon. This represents the unique part of the Nunavut year.

The star is the Niqirtsituq, the North Star which is the traditional guide for navigation and more broadly, forever remains unchanged as does the leadership of the elders in the community. The star is yellow on the blue

An *inuksuk* is a pile of stones stacked to look like a man. It is built as a landmark to guide people across the barren arctic landscape.

Research and appropriately colour the symbols.

Symbols of the Shield

(give the meanings of the symbols on the shield)

Star and Five Gold Circles:_____

_____

Inuit Stone Lamp:_____

_____

Inuksuk:_____

_____

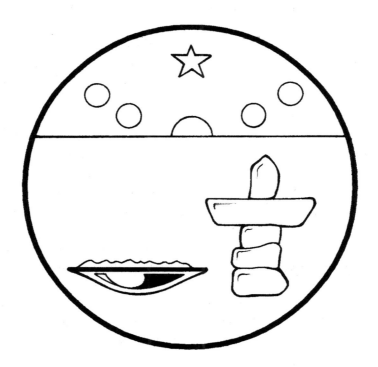

NUNAVUT

The frozen north is Canada's last frontier! This wild land of wilderness and endless coastline has yet unexplored bays and inlets. The two land groups are the Arctic mainland, and the Arctic Archipelago (islands). Nunavut contains four Canadian geological regions: The Canadian Shield, The Innutian Mountains, the Arctic Lowlands and the Hudson Bay Lowlands.

The Arctic mainland lies predominantly in the *Canadian Shield* region, with the bottom tip touching the *Hudson Bay Lowlands*. The bottom border of the territory basically follows the treeline, giving to Nunavut the exposed bedrock, lakes and moss covered hills which are bare or dotted with dwarf willow. This desolate place, called the Barren Lands, is mostly uninhabited except along the coast.

The low-lying islands to the north, part of the *Arctic Lowlands,* are frozen in sea-ice most of the year. The short summer brings a covering of moss and lichens to the land. Seventy percent of the island population live on Baffin, Victoria and King William Islands.

The eastern islands of Nunavut, Baffin Island and Ellesmere Island, include the rocky, snow-covered *Innutian Mountains*.

Most of Nunavut receives very little precipitation. In the northern islands of the Arctic Archipelago, temperatures never rise above freezing even in July. In the lower islands and along the mainland coast, the summer temperature averages only five to ten degrees above freezing. The weather is unpredictable and can delay air travel, hunting trips, and other activities. What do you think it means to be "weathered out?" The Nunavut residents use this term to say that bad weather has disrupted their plans.

The border between Nunavut and the Northwest Territories follows the traditional aboriginal dividing line between the Dene and Cree of the west, and the Inuit of the northeast. By following the treeline the border makes Nunavut the only territory with virtually no trees. Most of the territory is in the natural region called the Arctic Tundra.

North of 60

Look on a map to see how the border between the territories and the provinces lies along the 60th parallel of latitude. Residents of the territories call themselves "northerners" and say they live "North of 60." They call all others "southerners."

A large variety of seabirds nest along the coast, feeding on the swarms of mosquitoes and blackflies that torment the people of the land.

Whales, walrus, polar bears, seals, and caribou are the unique mammals that swim or roam around the Arctic islands.

Alert

On top of the world sits the most northerly permanent settlement in the world, Alert. Originally a weather station, it is now a military base. Alert is just 500 miles from the north pole and far above the last Inuit settlement. A sign there reads: "There is no place anything like this place, anywhere near this place, so this must be the place: Alert."

The Old Life was a long walk on an empty stomach.
Inuit expression quoted by Robin Gedalog, *Paper Stays Put; A Collection of Inuit Writing,* (1980).

Internet Links: Nunavut quizzes as **Fun Trivia**. Printable relief map of Nunavut at **Canada Info Link**. For these and more links go to Easylinks at **donnaward.net**

Geological Regions
Colour the land of each geological region a different colour.

Natural Regions
Nunavut lies in the Arctic Tundra region.

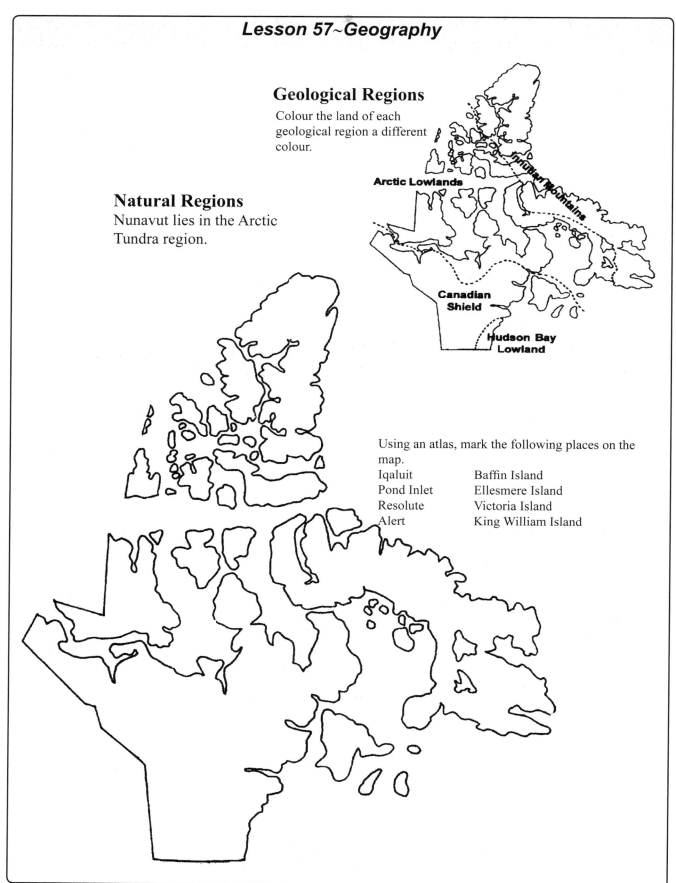

Arctic Lowlands

Innuitian Mountains

Canadian Shield

Hudson Bay Lowland

Using an atlas, mark the following places on the map.

Iqaluit	Baffin Island
Pond Inlet	Ellesmere Island
Resolute	Victoria Island
Alert	King William Island

Population

Nunavut: 26,745
Iqaluit: 5,236 (territorial capital)

Communications

The settlements in Nunavut are separated by vast distances and harsh winters. All but two communities are connected by telephone and radio. Radiophones link hunting camps with towns. A radio station broadcasting from Iqaluit, the capital of Nunavut, carries local news and even personal messages.

Iqaluit is at the end of Frobisher Bay on the south shore of Baffin Island. The largest of the twenty-eight settlements, Iqaluit is connected with the other settlements and the south only by airplane. An average of 45 flights travel each day in and out of Iqaluit.

There is only one 21 km stretch of government-maintained road in Nunavut. Most of the few community roads are unpaved. It is no wonder that there are more snowmobiles than cars or trucks in Nunavut.

Costly Food

Food prices are much higher than other places in Canada because of high transportation costs. Ships can only travel in and out of the ports for 12 weeks of the year.

In the remote areas of Nunavut you might pay $2 for one apple, or $5 for one litre of milk. Local people still rely on food from the land, however, there is now concern about toxins (poisons) found in seal meat and other marine mammals due to pollution which makes its way into arctic waters.

History Highlights

	Native peoples dwell in the land
1577	Martin Frobisher claims Baffin Island for the British in his search for the Northwest Passage.
1670	Hudson's Bay Co. is established and acquires Princes Rupert's Land
1848	John Franklin's expedition is frozen in Victoria Strait and lost
1880	Britain gives the Arctic Archipelago to the Dominion of Canada
1960	Inuit arts and crafts business gains momentum
1982	NWT voters approve the concept of Nunavut
1999	Nunavut becomes a self-governing territory

Change has come rapidly to northerners as the traditional lifestyle of hunting and fishing has become a memory rather than a lifestyle. The old way was very hard and there was far more hunger than today. Inuit now, however, struggle with different problems, such as idleness resulting in boredom, hopelessness, and despair. By taking charge of their lives again in the governing of their own land, the Inuit want to bring new hope to the young people.

Colour the population bar graph.
See library books on Nunavut (adult & children's library section 917.12).
Also: Bryan and Cherry Alexander. *The Inuit, Hunters of the North.* (1973).
Gedalog, Robin (ed.). *Paper Stays Put, A Collection of Inuit Writing.* (1980).

POPULATION BAR GRAPH

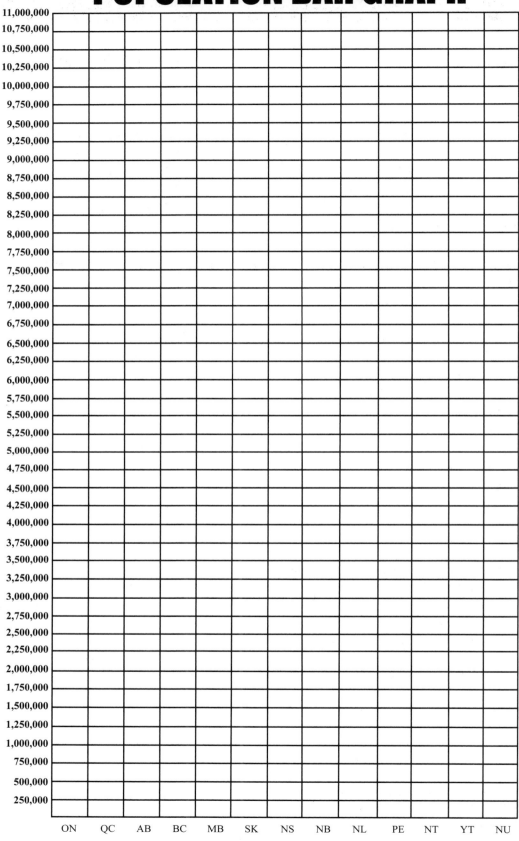

Note: These are the official postal abbreviations of the provinces and territories

126

Lesson 4, p. 11

1. Of the three questions listed, circle the one an *economist* would *not* ask. ⓒ

2. In the blank beside each sentence write: "P" if it describes a *primary* industry, "Sec" if it describes *secondary* industry, and "Ser" if it describes a *service* industry.

Sec At the National Sea Products factory in Lunenburg, N.S., fish sticks are made, and packaged in a box with the High Liner label.

P Across Canada, those in the timber trade not only harvest trees, but also finance replanting projects to provide timber for the next . . . .

Ser Computer software consultants help people learn or adapt computer programs to their business needs.

P When international oil prices rose dramatically in the 1970s it brought a real boost to oil producers in Alberta.

Ser As a large percentage of our population gets older, there will be greater need for workers in health care.

3. Match the definition:

Exports — products sold to other countries
Industry — the making of products
Economize — to make choices about spending
Imports — products bought from other countries
International trade — G & S exchanged between countries

4. If a country imported more goods than it exported, would this be good for the economy? Why?
If a country imported more goods than it exported, it would be buying more than it was selling. That sends money out of the country which is not good for the economy.

Lesson 12, p. 31

1. As an exporter of forestry products, in what place does Canada rank in the world?

a) third place b) (first place) c) fifth place d) tenth place

2. Is timber a renewable product or a non-renewable product? Explain why.
Timber is a renewable product as trees reproduce themselves. Forests however, do take a long time to grow.

3. In British Columbia environmentalists have clashed with the forest industry over what issue?
Environmentalists clash with lumber companies that cut "old growth" forests.

4. Match the process or product to the appropriate area of the forest industry.

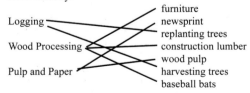

Logging — furniture, newsprint, replanting trees
Wood Processing — construction lumber, wood pulp
Pulp and Paper — harvesting trees, baseball bats

5. What two insects are very destructive to Canada's forests?
Two destructive insects are the spruce budworm and the pine bark beetle.

6. Name two reasons why forest fires can be good for a forest.
*1. Forest fires clear old wood to make space for new growth
2. Ash provides nutrients for new growth.
3. The black spruce and the lodgepole pine need fire to release the seeds from the cones.*

Lesson 16, p. 40

1. Name three reasons why Canada is a country which uses a lot of energy.
*1. Canadians need to heat buildings.
2. Canada is a large country and Canadians travel long distances.
3. Factories, mills and refineries use a great deal of energy.*

2. Name two non-renewable forms of energy.
Two forms of non-renewable energy are oil and coal (or natural gas).

3. Where is coal most often used now? Name three provinces where coal is mined.
Coal is most often used in manufacturing. Coal is mined in Saskatchewan, Alberta and B.C. (Also N.S. or N.B.).

4. From what two words was the term *petroleum* taken, and why? What is the term for petroleum today?
The word petroleum was taken from the Latin terms for rock and oil. Today it is called crude oil.

5. Name two reasons why natural gas is a good home fuel.
Natural gas is less expensive and cleaner burning than oil.

7. What two provinces contain offshore oil deposits?
Offshore oil deposits are found in Newfoundland and Nova Scotia.

8. How is your home heated? *Answers will vary.*

Lesson 20, p. 49

1. What is the percentage of Canadians who farm today? What makes it possible for so few to grow all the food Canadians need?
Three percent of Canadians farm. Large farms and specialized equipment make it possible for a few farmers to grow all the food Canadians need.

2. What four ingredients result in good farmland?
Four ingredients needed for good farmland are: adequate rain, fertile soil, level land, and warm days.

3. Name the four main kinds of farms.
The four main kinds of farms are: field crops, livestock, fruit and vegetable, and mixed farms.

4. Match a province to a type of farming important to that province. Although some provinces may have various kinds of farms, pick the one which most closely matches.

Alberta — Field Crops
Saskatchewan — Livestock - beef
Quebec — Livestock - dairy
Prince Edward Island — Vegetables
British Columbia — Fruit

Lesson 24, p. 58

1. For what reason were people from Japan and China restricted....? *People from Japan and China were restricted from immigrating because of racial prejudice.*

2. What are the three categories for immigrant status?
1) Family members in Canada 2) Job skills 3) Refugees

3. What changed in Canada with the Official Languages Act?
Canada became a bilingual country.

4. Name two things immigrants are encouraged to retain . . . .?
Immigrants are encouraged to retain their language & heritage.

5. Name both good results and negative results of multiculturalism.
Good: Positive self-identity, Negative: Isolation.

Lesson 28, p. 66

1. What are the three things they consider when choosing a site? *Manufacturers want a close location to 1) raw materials, 2) inexpensive transportation, and 3) large markets.*

2. The Golden Horseshoe is close to what route and large markets? *The Golden Horseshoe is close to the St. Lawrence and Great Lakes Seaway and markets of Ontario, Quebec and eastern United States.*

4. What is Ontario's most important primary industry and where are the largest of these industries located? *Ontario's most important primary industry is steel making, located at Hamilton and Sault Ste. Marie.*

Lesson 32, p. 74

1. How did early settlers use water to make power? What did they use the energy for? *Early settlers used water to turn water wheels which powered grist mills for grinding grain into flour, and saw mills for cutting logs.*

2. What invention made it possible to harness water to make hydroelectricity? *The invention of the generator made it possible to use water to make hydroelectricity.*

3. What natural feature in Canada allows the country to produce hydroelectricity? *Canada has many rivers suitable for producing hydroelectricity.*

4. Which province produces the most hydroelectricity and what is the name of the large hydroelectric project in that province? *The province of Quebec produces the most hydroelectricity. The James Bay Project is the large hydroelectric project in Quebec.*

5. Why will there be a continual push for power plant sites in the north? *There will be a continual push for northern sites because power plants close to the cities have become inadequate*

Lesson 36, p. 82

1. Write the number showing why each animal became endangered...

2	Sea Mink	1.	Loss of food
4	Peregine Falcon	2.	Trapping
1	Black-footed Ferret	3.	Loss of habitat
3	Whooping Crane	4.	Pollution

2. Write the following terms beside the appropriate description.

endangered The Vancouver I. marmot lives high in the mountains ....

extinct Funk Island, off the coast of Labrador, was once home to a flightless, penguin-like bird called the great auk....

vulnerable The Atlantic cod was once the most valuable catch on ....

extirpated The great bison of the plains once sustained the Plains ...

threatened The white beluga whale lives in arctic waters and a small ...

Lesson 40, p. 91

1. About how many years have fishing fleets fished the waters .... *Fleets have been fishing at Newfoundland for about 500 years.*

2. Match the definitions to the terms.
Food for small fish — raised area of the continental
Continental shelf — plankton
Bank — up to 200 meters
Plankton — small fish
Food for large fish — ocean floor 200 meters or less
Sunlight penetrates water — microscopic plants and animals

3. How does sport fishing benefit the economy? *Tourists spend money on equipment, lodging and food.*

4. What two factors make it difficult for fishers to count on a steady income? *Fishers have a hard time making a steady income because of changes in fish numbers and market prices.*

5. Make at least three comparisons between offshore trawlers and inshore fishers.

Offshore	Inshore
Large boats	Small boats
Remain at sea 2-3 weeks	Return home each night
Can fish in bad weather	Can't fish in bad weather
Sonar tracking equipment	No sonar
Run by large companies	Run by families

Lesson 44, p. 99

1. Tourists create jobs for Canadians by spending their money on what five things? *Tourists spend their money on transportation, accommodation, food, recreation, and entertainment.*

2. What percentage of tourism income comes from business travellers? *Business travellers contribute 50% of the tourism income.*

3. What kinds of things attract visitors to Canada? *Canada's attractions are the scenery, resources, recreation, and entertainment.*

4. Explain why it is **not** good for the economy if Canadians spend more money travelling outside of Canada than .... *It is not good for the economy for Canadians to spend their money in other countries because then the workers in our tourism industry do not benefit while those in other countries do.*

5. Name some places you would like to visit in Canada and tell why. *Answers will vary.*

Lesson 48, p. 107

1. What is rock called that contains high concentrations of a useful mineral? *Rock that contains high concentrations of a useful mineral is called ore.*

2. What are the three groupings of minerals? *Minerals are grouped into metallics, non-metallics and fossil fuels.*

3. Match the terms.
Precious metals — metals mixed
Base metals — materials used in con.
Alloy — sand and gravel
Aggregate — gold and silver
Structural minerals — quartz and salt
Nonmetallic minerals — iron, zinc and copper

4. Why is underground mining more expensive than open-pit mining? *Underground mining is more expensive because of the drilling and safety structures required.*

5. In what areas do mining companies restore open-pit sites? *Mining companies restore sites close to settled areas.*

Internet Links: Provincial Quiz at **Historica**. Go to Teaching and Learning/Student Games. Fun Symbols game for review. Provincial Flowers Quiz at **Fun Trivia**. Easylinks at **donnaward.net**